MOMMA'S OLIVE BRANCH

Momma's Olive Branch

A true story

Elizabeth Tisdale Armstrong

To order additional copies of this book, contact:
Xlibris Corporation
1-888-795-4274
www.Xlibris.com
Orders@Xlibris.com
52914

CHAPTER ONE

Imagine growing up in a place where time seems to stand still, a place where history and tradition hover like a blanket over a town, creating a feeling of comfort and importance. In the heart of town, large gnarled but graceful old trees grow along the cobblestone-lined streets. Beside frame houses, there are white picket fences surrounding gardens full of brightly colored flowers. Birds twitter high up in the trees. The skies are not always so clear, but often are a vivid blue with ball-like white cotton clouds. Often there is a faint smell of wood smoke in the air from a working fire. Sometimes there is a smell of fresh gingerbread, or the spicy smell of curing meat. Along with the birds, the sounds of metal carriage wheels mixed with the *clop clop* of horse hooves can be heard moving along the streets. Voices, cheerful and excited, echo through the streets as groups of people move about the town—looking, imagining, learning about an era gone by in most other parts of our country. But here it still seems to continue, bringing with it a sort of magic message. "The past is important to the future," it whispers to those who are willing to listen. I, as a child, listened and learned.

The town I grew up in is Williamsburg, Virginia. The restored area, started by men named Rockefeller and Godwin some twenty years prior to my birth, was in its prime in the 1960s, when I was a little girl. Archeology played a larger role then than it does now. So many things were still being unearthed and discovered. The town had such a tingling, excited feeling all the time. It was like we all had this huge diamond mine and wanted to share a little piece of it to every visitor who came in town.

My father worked for the Colonial Williamsburg Foundation. He was an audio-visual engineer and worked on films and recordings that documented both the history of the town and the archeological findings of the foundation. I especially remember when excavation work was going on to restore the old Weatherburn's Tavern. Some old wine bottles had been found in an archeological dig behind the building, and some of the bottles still had cherry wine in them! It was such an exciting time for everyone who worked for the foundation. We were like one big family, and each new discovery was felt as a success for us all.

There were other things that made this town important to me. From the time I was very little, my mother would take me on walks through the many flower gardens and down to the duck pond behind the Governor's Palace. I was drawn to flowers before I was even able to walk and talk! So many of my baby pictures show me holding a flower in my fist. My father participated in the demonstrations of how soldiers used muskets and would parade down the main street with the fife and drum corps. I vividly remember the loud beating of the drums in my ears and how it felt like my heartbeat echoed the drum's pounding in the middle of my chest. My brothers and I used to go for bike rides down the main street, called the Duke of Gloucester Street, and dodge in and out of groups of tourists. Perhaps most important of all, our family attended church in the old historic Bruton Parish, which has always been a living church since the 1700s, steeped in tradition and pride in its history. That was my favorite spot in the whole town. I knew every inch of the graveyard and what parts of the building were original and which were restored. I always was fascinated by the supposed place where Thomas Jefferson carved his name in the balcony as a young man attending the College of William and Mary.

My mother encouraged my brothers and me to sing in the church choir, which we did from second through twelfth grades, and my mother sang in the adult choir. Daddy would have loved to have been a part of a choir, but as he always put it, he couldn't carry a tune in a bucket. He was content to watch and listen, and he contributed his time and talents to the Sunday school department. Sitting up in the choir stalls, close to the altar, I always felt closer to God. With the huge brass chandelier full of glowing candles hanging overhead, there was such a sense of majesty and holiness. It made me tingle at the thought of being a part of that.

So for me growing up, history and tradition were a way of life in family and business. My father didn't make a huge living, but he was the best at what he did, and many admired his work. As an audio-visual engineer for the foundation, he helped make the recordings for educational films about eighteenth-century life, and he made the many records about various eighteenth-century music that the foundation put out each year. I always thought he should have been paid more, but we were comfortable, and we were very rich in love. I have vivid memories of what Daddy was like at work—very focused as he listened for any imperfections in a recording. Lines like "Testing, one, two, three" always make me think of him. He had no tolerance for a poor recording, and he would expound upon the subject quite openly and fiercely.

He didn't like for anyone to "eat" a microphone. A little went a long way, he said. But when a recording went well for him, he swelled with pride. He would do that funny little whistle between his teeth and tap his foot in time to the music. That's how I remember him the most.

As a child, I loved to hear the story of how my parents had met almost as much as my father enjoyed telling it. Daddy would always get a sparkle in his blue eyes as he related the facts. Momma would listen quietly, smiling, and only interrupt to correct him every once in a while. It began in the spring of 1956. Momma had moved to the big city of Richmond, Virginia, to teach. She worked at Highland Springs High School in Henrico County and taught English, French, and journalism. She was very well liked by her students. She shared an apartment with a fellow teacher named Frances. Frances began dating a young man she had met at the local radio station, WRVA. His name was Irby Hollins, and he loved telling the girls stories of the things that went on down at the radio station. Irby frequently would tell my mother that she should meet one of his coworkers, Dick Tisdale. Irby said he was a real swell guy with a great sense of humor. My mother declined, but eventually, Irby and Frances cooked up a way for the two of them to meet. Irby scheduled a tour of the radio station for both my mother and Frances. While there, my father caught a glimpse of my mother from down the hall and immediately wanted to know who she was. "That is the woman I plan to marry!" he boasted. Irby made sure the two met, and eventually they began dating. After a few months, my father asked my mother to marry him, but she refused, saying they needed to get to know one another better. Daddy continued asking her from time to time, but always she refused. Secretly, she was waiting for him to propose to her on Valentine's Day. When he did, she at last said the "yes" he was waiting to hear. They were married a little over a year later in April of 1958.

It wasn't especially unusual that my parents developed such a close-knit family. My mother came from a very close family, and when she married my father, they took him in as though he had always been a part of it. Daddy was an only child, and his mother doted on him. I never was able to really know my paternal grandparents. He died two months after I was born, which sent my grandmother into a depressive state. I was about four and a half when she died; I have a very shadowy image of her in my mind, but I never developed a real relationship with her. Losing his parents hurt my father deeply. Daddy didn't cry often, but the few times I remember him crying were because he missed his parents. It was usually at Christmas when he missed them the most. Daddy loved Christmas better than anyone I have ever known. His excitement about the holiday was so catching, and to see him suddenly break down and cry at such a happy time made quite an impression on me as a young child. I remember once telling him that I never wanted to be like him in that one way, missing my parents at Christmastime. How ironic.

But my mother's family provided so much love and caring, it never bothered me that I only had one set of living grandparents. I remember taking those long trips to the mountains of Virginia to visit them. The trip seemed to take forever as we would wind along state roads heading for the mountains of Virginia. We would always get a more excited feeling as the tops of the mountains began to come into view near Charlottesville. You could begin to see their bluish purple outlines, and the road began to wind more. We always broke up the trip by taking a picnic lunch to eat at the top of Afton Mountain. We used a picnic area designed for travelers near the top of the mountain. The benches were a bit rustic and stained, and you could hear the rush of traffic as cars continued on their journeys. But the air smelled sweeter and felt cooler there. The view below to the valley was like a peek at the world from heaven. You could see specks of tiny white houses nestled among masses of green trees, sloping down the mountain into the valley. But Daddy wouldn't let us linger too long. Anxious to continue on, he would usher us all back to the car after eating.

From that point, the trip had about three more hours left before we would arrive in Christiansburg, Virginia, where my grandparents lived. Christiansburg is a small town nestled near the top of a small mountain, appropriately named Christiansburg Mountain. It is about thirty minutes past Roanoke and uphill all the way. As the car would begin its climb up Christiansburg Mountain, an excited feeling would fill the whole car. Momma and Daddy were just as anxious to arrive as we children were! "We're almost there," my mother would sing out. Finally, we would exit the highway and drive into the little town. The house sat perched on the side of a slope right beside the town hall. We could hardly contain ourselves as Daddy pulled into the driveway. He always tooted the horn to signal our arrival, but it wasn't always necessary. My grandparents were usually waiting up on the front porch, waving hello. We couldn't wait to jump out of the car and bound up the steps to those open arms.

Times at my grandparents' house were filled with laughter and lots of visiting. Friends of the family and distant cousins would drop by when they heard we were there. We would fill the hours with talking and catching up on what had happened since the last visit. Food was another thing there was always plenty of. I remember fresh tomatoes, both yellow and red; fried chicken; homemade ice cream; and homemade chocolate syrup, the kind that gets chewy when it hits that cold ice cream! And fresh homemade bread. No one could make bread or rolls like my grandmother, and she always had fresh breads either coming out of or going into the oven, with more on the counter, rising. The delicious smells coming from the kitchen always filled the whole house. She also made all kinds of jams and pimento cheese spread and pound cake to die for. She canned yellow cherries she picked from a tree in her backyard, and they were my favorite. She always seemed to have an apron on, and she always smelled so good, like rising bread. She often whistled or hummed a tune as she worked in the kitchen. I've never known anyone else who had a merry twinkle in their eyes like my grandmother's. She had a deep, stubborn determination too. She waged a war against Japanese beetles that ate her prize roses. She would carry an old tin can of scalding, hot water to the garden each morning, pick the beetles off the blossoms, and throw them in the tin can. The beetles wiggled and struggled, thrashing about in the hot water. Then she would carry them into the house and flush them down the toilet! She also hated crows and blackbirds eating seeds in her yard. She thought they frightened off other birds like robins, cardinals, and bluebirds, which she loved watching. She had a big black cap gun she would shoot off in the backyard, and she would shout, "Go away, you old grackles!" It was quite a sight to see—this small-framed older woman with a gentle, lovely face and brown hair with few silver streaks twisted into a bun on her head, wielding a cap pistol at a bunch of birds. But it seemed to work.

My grandfather was a quiet man in contrast to my grandmother. But they complemented each other so well. He never raised his voice, but still commanded respect and admiration. He was held in high regard by all that knew him in the town of Christiansburg. He was a man of honor and integrity, who could be counted on in both good and tough times. He too had a sweet face that almost always wore a smile. His dark eyes held the look of wisdom and kindness. He often puffed on a stump of a cigar, and he had a little chuckle that shook his plump tummy when he laughed. My grandparents had a very strong bond of love, which showed in every aspect of how they lived their lives. They passed it on to friends and strangers, but most especially to their four children.

My mother had two brothers and one sister. Uncle B., as he was called by his nieces and nephews, was the eldest, eleven years older than my mother. He never married but preferred instead to travel and study music. He had settled in Philadelphia and became a beloved teacher at the Conservatory of Music there. He spent most of his summers with my grandparents. I adored him from the time I was a very little girl, and I sensed that I held a special place in his heart as well. He sometimes traveled to Europe for a few weeks out of the summer, mostly Germany, and also Canada, and he always brought back special treasures for me. One of my favorites was a tiny clock with delicate pink and lavender flowers painted on it. He taught me German phrases, and I loved to hear his thick accent. I would giggle and giggle when he threw up his hands in mock exasperation and say, *"Och die Liebe des himmels!"* or *"Gott segne euch!"* when I sneezed. He would sit me up on his lap and sing songs or tell me fantastic stories. He would help me play "Chopsticks" on the piano. When I grew a bit older, my grandfather built a doll's house for me. Uncle B. made doll furniture for the house, and we would spend hours decorating each room together. It was at about this time that he gave me *The Chronicles of Narnia* to read. They were some of the most wonderful books I'd ever read. And Uncle B.'s dressing closet, off the room where he slept in my grandparents' house, had the most curious wardrobe sitting at the back of it. It looked exactly like the one described in the book *The Lion, the Witch, and the Wardrobe.* I can't look at that wardrobe today without a shiver coming over me.

Next in line was my Aunt Bettie, six years younger than Uncle B. She had inherited the vibrant personality of my grandmother. She had studied at the University of Virginia to become a nurse anesthetist. She was considered one of the best in her field until being diagnosed with multiple sclerosis not too long before I was born. I don't remember a time when she was out of a wheelchair. But I also don't remember hearing her complain or grumble about her situation. She was married to a doctor, my Uncle Robbie. He was a tall, thin quiet figure who took good care of her but remained distant from our family, never really making an effort to fit in with us. Aunt Bettie had a housekeeper from Bolivia named Gladys. I loved her strong accent and bold Latin personality. Aunt Bettie was unable to have children of her own, so she had a dog. Susie was a big black Lab, who was severely spoiled rotten. Aunt Bettie also delighted in spoiling her nieces and nephews. She would send us little presents and cards with stickers. I remember her as such a good example of living life to the fullest no matter what circumstances befall you.

The last two children were twins, my mother and my Uncle Don. My Uncle Don became a Baptist minister and was always very busy. He married my Aunt Kay when I was two years old. My mother sang in their wedding. I have a fuzzy memory of her wearing a gold choir robe, looking like an angel in the choir loft. Uncle Don and Aunt Kay didn't start their family right away, so as a little girl, I didn't feel as close to them. It wasn't until I was about nine years old that the first of my two cousins was born, and we began to bond more strongly. Uncle Don was always charming and charismatic. He was a fantastic storyteller, and he was full of funny anecdotes or rhymes. He seized the moment frequently to make a rhyme or a pun. I remember lines like "Mabel, Mabel, sweet and able, get your elbows off the table!" "Better listen to your dad, or you'll make him awfully mad!" and "Off to bed, you sleepyhead!" He would often send my brothers and me into gales of laughter. Aunt Kay was quieter and a bit shy sometimes. She was very pretty, with beautiful pale skin that blushed pink when she felt flustered or embarrassed. For as long as I've known her, she has always had an air of grace and sweetness about her, like an angel. She and I have grown quite close over the years, and I think of her as probably the most perfect person I know.

The family gathering place at the house in Christiansburg was the big front porch. I liked sitting on the glider swing with my grandfather. He would gently rock the swing with his foot as he puffed quietly on a cigar. The rocking motion would put me in a trancelike state, and I sat there in total contentment, listening to the others talk. My relatives would relate such fabulous stories about times past. There was laughter, so much laughter, and you knew deep in your bones that this was the closest you could get to heaven on earth. You felt so safe . . . so content . . . so perfect. When we enjoyed the porch in the daytime, we would bird-watch or count the cars as they came down the hill in front of the house and stopped at the traffic light at the bottom. The bus station was directly across the street, and we would watch the people getting off and speculate about where they were going and why. Uncle B. was especially good at that game. He would make up the wildest, funniest stories about where each person from the bus might have been going. He could make me giggle for hours, it seemed. Often the fire siren would sound off, and we would watch the fire trucks race off to a fire or car accident. My brothers especially loved watching the fire trucks. I always covered my ears as tightly as I could to block the loud screeching sound. At night we would count the fireflies and listen to the music of the crickets or listen for the faint hoot of an owl. Those were golden times our family spent up in the mountains with my grandparents.

I had the privilege of being the firstborn and the only daughter. I was the only grandchild too for four years. I was spoiled, of course, but mostly in a good way. I remember afternoons of my mother reading *Winnie the Pooh* to me. We often took walks together in the gardens of Colonial Williamsburg and fed ducks or chased guinea hens or watched sheep grazing. We always smelled the flowers in the gardens when they were in bloom. My favorites were the tulips. Momma would let me help her with cooking and baking in the kitchen. As I got older, she taught me how to sew and how to knit and crochet. She saw I had a creative talent, and she pinched pennies to enroll me in a pastel drawing class. She always treated me like I was her best friend. No matter what I did, good or bad, she made sure I knew I was loved and that I was special.

Sometimes Daddy took me to his office and would show me his sound equipment. I liked going into Daddy's boss's office and shaking Mr. Smith's hand. He would always let me choose a treat from the candy bowl in his office. Sometimes Daddy would take me to the college concerts he had to record at William and Mary. I loved watching him work. Sometimes at home, he would put on a classical record and let me ballet-dance to the music. He would help me twirl around and around. He always made me feel just like a princess. That was one of his pet names for me, Princess.

Once my brothers came along, I don't remember much of a feeling of less time with my parents as I do a feeling of shared time with my parents. I was the big sister they called Sissy. My parents let me know that was a very important job, one that they had every faith in me of performing well. That is not to say that there was no typical sibling rivalry, but mostly, we got along well and shared. We would all climb up on my parents' bed together, and Momma would read about King Arthur or Uncle Remus stories to us. In the summer, Momma went with us to the swimming pool to sit through three sets of swimming lessons. She always found time to make new clothes for me. She often was the room mother for our classes at school. She took us to the public library and helped us choose good books. Reading was one of her greatest loves, and she taught us to love books too.

Daddy taught me how to ride my bike. Once he helped me paint a poster for a contest in fourth grade. He pushed us on the swings. He made wooden trucks for my brothers and an outside playhouse for me in our backyard. There is so much good to remember. The rough times are greatly overshadowed by those wonderful times.

Being the oldest allowed me to have a very special relationship with both my parents, but I became especially close to my mother when Daddy began to get sick. She confided her fears to me and leaned on me for support and help with my two younger brothers. I remember her often saying that God had a purpose in giving her a daughter first. My mother would talk to me often about how she felt. I knew she wanted to go back to college and get a masters degree in library science. She wanted to be an elementary school librarian. She didn't think she would enjoy teaching English anymore because she said she felt she couldn't relate to "today's teens." She loved books and reading. As I got older and older, I noticed that she spent more time reading a book than anything else. It was an escape for her from all the pressures of Daddy's illnesses, and eventually her own illness too

After Donald, the youngest, was born, Daddy's health first began to suffer. I was only six, but I remember times of him being in and out of the hospital. He suffered from several different things: poor circulation, phlebitis, and eventually, diabetes. I remember that a nurse who lived on our street came over every day for about a month, teaching Daddy how to give himself insulin shots. He practiced on an orange, which my brothers and I thought was funny. At the same time, I thought my dad was very brave to be able to give himself shots. I knew I would never be able to do such a thing.

By the time I was in the ninth grade, diabetes had taken its toll on my father's circulatory system. His left leg had such poor circulation it had huge open sores that wouldn't heal. I know my mother worried terribly about him. She had tried so much to help him get better, watching his diet and his salt intake, buying support socks, going with him on evening walks in the neighborhood to exercise, even borrowing my Aunt Bettie's whirlpool machine for the bathtub. Nothing was helping my father's poor circulation, and the doctors were becoming more and more concerned. There was a fear that Daddy would lose his leg.

CHAPTER TWO

But in early 1976, one of my father's doctors wanted to try a new procedure. He proposed that Daddy undergo circulatory vein replacement surgery. It was all very state-of-the-art at the time, and we felt very important that they wanted to try it out on my dad. They would take a portion of a large blood vein from Dad's upper right leg or hip and use it to replace the poorly damaged vein in Daddy's lower left leg, below the knee. I'm sure my parents were very worried, but I don't remember any of that. I just remember that they went ahead with the procedure, and it was very successful.

Daddy began to feel healthier and happier than he had for a long time. The skin on Daddy's leg grew pink and healthy again. The sores healed, and Daddy walked with a spring in his step he had not had in a long time. He lost his temper less often than before because he wasn't in pain constantly. He began to do things he hadn't felt like doing, such as tinkering with our car. That was what he was doing one late February afternoon in 1976. It changed the course of our lives.

I was sitting at my sewing machine, working on a dress I wanted to wear to the Valentine's Day dance at my high school that same evening. My brothers were out playing, and Momma was fixing dinner. It was a warm afternoon for February. I could hear shouts of children playing outside and birds chirping as I worked busily in my bedroom. I always seemed to try to take on too much at the last minute. My stubborn nature made me even more determined to get the dress finished in time to wear it that night. I had designed the dress myself. It was more grown-up than the one I had worn the year before. My mother had made that one, and although I liked it a lot and felt I looked good in it, I wanted to look more sophisticated and appealing to the boys. The dress my mother had made seemed too girlish to me, with its sweet little pink and white hearts on a white background and long sleeves and a simple rounded neckline. I had chosen a white satin fabric with blue and red pinstripes to make into a halter-style evening gown. In my mind's eye, I envisioned myself turning a few heads at this dance.

I could hear the sounds of Momma making dinner in the kitchen. The aroma of food cooking filled the house and made my stomach growl. It smelled like her spaghetti. She made the best sauce from scratch. Its spicy smell tickled my nose as I took a deep breath. I looked at the clock beside my bed. It was after four thirty already. Time was running short, and I sighed as I surveyed what was left for me to do on the dress. I was having trouble with the neckline. I wanted it to be just right, and the satiny material kept slipping as I worked with it. But I pushed on, never considering giving up. I was sure I would finish it in time to wear by seven o'clock.

Momma must have stopped what she was doing in the kitchen to go ask my dad a question, like "What vegetables do you want tonight, dear?" or "How much longer will you be working on the car?" My mother often would talk to Daddy as he tinkered with our car. And it was such a pretty afternoon—so sunny it felt more like April than February. Momma might have just wanted to enjoy the weather with Daddy before the sun sank, bringing the cold air back again. Whatever it was that caused her to go talk to him, she was standing right there beside him, between the front of the house and the front of the car, when he touched the wrong part of the car by accident. I was still sewing in my room, concentrating very hard on getting the halter ties the right length on my dress.

As I worked carefully, pinning the seams just right and daydreaming of how lovely I thought I would look twirling on the dance floor, my mind was a million miles away when I heard the loudest crash I'd ever heard before. *What in the world?* I thought, and I stopped and frowned, listening. I heard something but was unsure of what it was at first. Was it a scream? It seemed more like a wailing sound unlike any I ever heard before. I put the dress down and listened more closely. It had such an animal-like quality to it. In disgust at being interrupted, I got up from the chair and walked down the hallway toward the front of the house. I was thinking, *What have my brothers gotten into now?* But suddenly as I walked closer to the front of the house, I realized it was no animal or child at all. My heart leapt to a halt in my chest as if an icy hand had grabbed it through my very skin. My mother! It was my mother screaming! It was a guttural, terrified scream the likes of which I had never heard before in my life. The realization that something horrible and serious had happened sent me into a panicked run.

That was the first time I remember those little fireworks going off inside my head as I ran in terror to see what had happened. They are a very familiar sensation to me now that I am older, but at that time, I had never known such fear. The scene before me was rather calm under the circumstances, of which I would later learn. I saw my parents, lying on their backs in the driveway. Daddy's face was as pale and white as a full moon. Momma was pale too, but she was just screaming and screaming and wouldn't stop. The front of our house was bowed in from the force of being struck. Some of the siding boards were splintered and chipped. My little brother, Donald, was standing not too far away from my parents, wringing his hands and looking like a scared rabbit. Daddy yelled something to him, and I watched Donald run over to the car and turn it off. Daddy slumped back in a heap on the ground and was very still. Momma was still screaming and moaning. I didn't comprehend it all immediately, but what had happened was that Daddy had touched something, activating the throttle while the engine was running, which caused the car to lurch forward. In a few fleeting seconds, the car had pinned my parents up against the front of our house and then bounced back again. Petrified that the car would lunge forward again, my father had yelled to the only person he saw, eight-year-old Donald, to turn off the key in the ignition. I remember standing there saying "Oh my god" over and over without realizing I was saying it too much. It was like being stuck in your own bad dream, but you are wide awake.

Everything moved in slow motion . . . everything but my heart. The sound of my pulse beating in my ears was deafening. I screamed for Richard, my other brother, but he wasn't around. I couldn't seem to come up with a single rational thought. My mind felt like a computer on the brink of crashing. Suddenly, there was our neighbor Emily Richardson from across the street. I focused on her lovely, kind face. Everything else blurred around me. Her voice was clear and calm. She spoke slowly. She told me to get blankets to cover my parents because their warmth would keep away shock. Giving me that task helped me to focus. I put my all into finding every blanket I could in that house. Back and forth I ran, several times, bringing blankets to cover my parents. I would bring them out, and someone else, I don't remember who, took them from me so I could run back for more. I briefly noticed that there were many people in my front yard, helping, but I didn't stop to see who exactly they were. I continued with my blanket mission.

At one point, I noticed more blankets were put on my mother than on my dad. I recall feeling annoyed about that and started to go get another blanket just for my dad. But the ambulance arrived, and I was asked to stand aside. It was only then that I really noticed how many people were standing in my yard and who they were. Neighbors had come out of their houses to see what was going on. Groups of children were gathered, looking at the ambulance. I noticed that Richard was finally there, standing beside Donald and watching. He had a pained, lost look of bewilderment on his face. Donald was on the verge of tears. The paramedics began to work on my parents. For the first time, I realized that the warm, springlike day was fading, and the cool air was nipping at me. My fingers were very cold, and so were my toes and my ears and the tip of my nose. The sun was starting to go down, and long shadows were cast onto the ground. I watched the paramedics load my parents into the ambulance. I wanted to go along, but they didn't allow it. I felt so lost and alone too as they closed the ambulance doors and drove away. At the same time, it was like a heavy weight was set on my shoulders. I knew I would have to be strong for my brothers. *But how can I be strong when I feel so small and lost?* I wondered. *What should we do next?*

One of my mom's best friends went to the hospital to be with her. Our close neighbors got together and decided how my brothers and I would be cared for that night. I helped a neighbor call my

Uncle Don, who lived the closest to us, only a couple hours away. He made plans to come as soon as possible. After that, there wasn't much we could do but sit and wait. It would be a while before we would get news of how my parents were doing and if one or both of them would be able to come home that night. It was decided that I should attend the school dance anyway. I really didn't want to. But my good friend, Linda, wanted me to go with her. I hadn't quite finished the dress I had been sewing. It still lay across my sewing chair in my bedroom. I decided I could still wear the one Momma had made for the Valentine's dance the year before. I didn't really feel much like wearing an alluring evening gown now anyway. So that was what I did. It was comforting to wear the dress that Momma had made for me. Weeks ago, when I had decided it was too young-looking for me to wear, I would have never guessed that I would be glad to wear it for that same reason now. It made me feel closer to Momma. I was still her little girl, and as long as I needed her, she would be around to take care of me, of us. She would be all right. I just had to be strong, I kept telling myself.

I didn't have a great deal of fun at that dance, but looking back, I think it was good that I went. Everyone seemed to know about what had happened, and many asked me about my parents and how I was doing. Even under those circumstances, such attention was good for an awkward teenager. I remember being so surprised that so many kids knew what had happened and seemed to care about my feelings. I usually wasn't the recipient of that kind of attention from my peers.

When Linda's mom picked us up from the dance, she had news of my parents. Momma was going to be able to come home right away. She was only badly bruised; amazingly, nothing was broken. Daddy, on the other hand, had suffered two broken legs. The damage to his newly repaired leg wasn't promising. Doctors were worried that he would end up losing the leg now. It would be a wait-and-see situation.

I couldn't wait to get home. Richard and Donald were going to spend the night with friends, but I would be at home with my mom to help her. She wasn't there when I got home, so I had plenty of time to change clothes and survey the damage to the house. The force of the car's impact had bowed the wall of our den inward a foot or so. My father had made beautiful wooden cabinets all along the back of that particular wall years before. We stored such things as board games, books, and records inside the cabinets. Now those things were strewn about the room as the blow from the car had catapulted them from their place. It was amazing to see what that car had done in such a short distance. My parents were lucky that their injuries hadn't been any worse. If I hadn't been prepared to see the damage to my home, I really wasn't prepared for the state that my mother returned home in. She had been so badly bruised that she couldn't walk. Her legs were all purple and swollen. It took two male neighbors to lift her from the car and get her into the house and into bed. She couldn't even handle crutches yet. The hospital had lent her a wheelchair for a week. I felt bad for what I felt was a humiliating experience for my mother. She may not have considered it that way at all, but I thought she must have felt uncomfortable having to have others lift her and carry her places. She hurt too much to even walk to the bathroom and had to use a bedpan. But through all her pain and possible humiliation, she worried about my father. I remember very vividly, after everyone had left and we were alone, I sat next to her on the bed as she cried out her worries to me. I had never seen her cry so much before. Her face looked so tired and worn. She had dark, purplish circles under her eyes. Her hands, with the perfectly manicured nails, were shaking as she spoke. What if he didn't make it? How would she go on without him? She was so afraid that he wouldn't be all right. I tried to comfort her as best I could.

When I had been five years old, I had to have my tonsils taken out. My mother had stayed in the hospital room with me. That had been the most comforting thing. Now in some small way, I was able to give a little bit back to her. I didn't cry. I listened and soothed her, telling her everything would be all right. I told her she could count on me. I would be strong enough for all of us, I said.

Over the next two weeks, my family worked toward trying to put our lives back in order. The insurance company began preparations for repairing the damaged wall. A lot of attention was given to my brother Donald. Everyone who heard or knew of the accident was impressed at how one so young could calmly and efficiently turn off the car ignition in such a crisis. His Cub Scout leader held a special award ceremony at the next pack meeting. Donald was given a plaque for bravery. A photo of him accepting the award appeared in the local newspaper.

The accident had happened about a week before Donald's eighth birthday. Momma had already planned a big party for him. She heard that the library sponsored a magician for birthday parties and provided the room and the decorations. We would supply the refreshments. Momma had arranged everything but the cake, which she had planned to make. I decided to take on that task. I don't remember why we chose a Washington's Birthday theme, except that it was February, but I decorated the cake with the face of George Washington. It looked remarkably like him! The party was wonderful. A couple of our close neighbors helped, and Donald didn't seem to notice that his parents weren't there helping him celebrate. We took lots of photographs, and Donald had a big smile in every one of them.

As so much improved over the next two weeks, the only thing that didn't was Daddy's left leg. It got worse. The doctors had given the leg a two-week period to begin to show signs of healing. They put the leg in a partial cast so they could continually check its progress. The other leg was in a full cast. The problem was that Daddy's new circulatory vein had been so badly crushed; it wasn't recovering. Blood wasn't circulating properly to allow the leg to heal, and by the end of two weeks, gangrene was starting to set in. Just when our family was beginning to recover from a horrible ordeal, we had to help our father cope with the impending loss of a limb. It was not really a decision. It *had* to be done to save his life. I know that it was a hard reality for my dad to face. He had been so optimistic about the special surgery to save his leg months earlier. And that surgery had gone so well and had been so successful. I know he carried a lot of guilt that it was his own fault for touching the wrong part on the car. He said himself that he knew better, and he didn't know what caused him to be so careless. But all that really didn't matter anymore. We needed to make our dad better, and he would still be the same man, just minus one leg. My mother made it very clear that she would love him no matter what, and so two weeks after what we have come to call *the car accident*, Daddy's left leg was amputated.

In the weeks following that surgery, Daddy would remark about how much healthier he felt. He hadn't realized how much the leg had pulled him down and drained him of energy. He could move around rather quickly on crutches. Eventually, he would be fitted for a temporary prosthesis as they formed a permanent one designed specifically for him. He affectionately nicknamed it George and joked that if he ever had to have his other leg removed, he would call that one Martha. Because of his diabetes, that scenario was a possibility in the far distant future.

Our lives began to go back to a more normal routine once again. The bicentennial year of 1976 was a big one in Williamsburg. Of course, the whole country was celebrating; but the Colonial Williamsburg Foundation wanted to lead the pack, so to speak, since much of what our country has become began right in our little town so long ago. Daddy returned to work and became very busy and involved in several foundation projects. In my eyes, the only real change was that Daddy's walk had a slight limp to it. That part was the most obvious to the outside world. But in the privacy of our home, even when Daddy took off the prosthesis, the horror of what we had all been through didn't come rushing back at us. It was just our new way of life. He was still every bit our dad, and we accepted the change very easily because Daddy was still with us. That was what was most important. My parents also decided to add on an additional bedroom and bath to our house—one that was wheelchair accessible. We all became enthralled with the exciting plans of the addition of a large master suite. It meant that all of us had our own bedrooms, and the boys no longer had to share a room.

That particular year, Amtrak Rails had a new train, which traveled the East Coast and was called the *Spirit of '76*. Momma and Daddy, together with Uncle B., arranged for my brothers and me to ride the train by ourselves from Williamsburg to Philadelphia, where Uncle B. lived, and visit for one week. As the oldest, I was in charge. It was a thrilling opportunity for a fifteen-year-old. Uncle B. took us to so many interesting places like the art museum and Independence Hall. We drove through the Amish country and up to Hershey, Pennsylvania, where we enjoyed a thrilling day at Hershey Park. We went through the battlefields of Gettysburg. I'm sure my Uncle B. was worn out after a week of entertaining three children, but it is a trip I will never forget.

CHAPTER THREE

As we grew in the richness of what our parents were able to provide, and as Daddy made remarkable progress toward a life that was as close to normal as possible again, circumstances began to set themselves up for another blow to our family. We didn't know that my mother was beginning to experience some warning signs from her body. She ignored them at first, too involved with Daddy's recovery and caring for three children. I have no idea exactly when she noticed things weren't quite right, or how long she ignored those signals. It was about a year after Daddy lost his leg that Momma was diagnosed with cervical cancer. Ironically, that type of cancer has one of the highest cure rates, but that's when it is discovered early. By the time she went to her doctor, she was experiencing heavy bleeding. Doctors feared it had probably already begun to spread to other parts of her body through the lymph nodes.

It was very surprising to me when my parents sat me down to explain that my mother had cancer. In the past, it had always been Daddy's health we were concerned about. It felt strange to be worrying about Momma in the same way. I have spent a lot of time reflecting on what happened and asking *why*. I have kept up with developments in cancer research and the progress made over these twenty-some years. I can't help but wonder if the trauma of the car accident triggered my mother's body to begin a growth of cancer, or whether it would have happened anyway. There is a side of me that understands how she could have put off going to the doctor. Now that I am a wife and mother, I see very well how in caring for your family, it is easy to put your own needs aside. It becomes second nature to put yourself last and procrastinate in doing things for yourself. But another side of me is still frustrated and hurt that she didn't go to the doctor sooner than she did. "If only" can be a difficult thing to live with.

After that diagnosis, life in our family became focused on Momma's recovery. That was difficult for me sometimes because I was in high school, and my thoughts were of becoming an adult and finding the direction I wanted my life to go in. But somehow, my parents managed to keep up with a relatively normal life for us. My brothers and I attended school as usual. We still participated in after-school activities. Richard played on a soccer team, and both he and Donald continued in the Boy Scouts. I became very involved in the drama club at my high school. The sponsored teacher was a kind of mentor for me. And all three of us continued to sing in the church choir together. Momma did as well when she felt up to it. My mother spent more and more of her time at the library, researching her disease. My dad had to take more time off from work than ever before, for reasons other than his own health. Trips to Richmond, Virginia, became commonplace. That was where the closest cancer research hospital was, at the Medical College of Virginia.

That first summer of my mother's battle with cancer was a difficult one. She had to have extensive and frequent radiation treatments. Living sixty miles away from the cancer hospital did not allow for this, so Momma had to live in Richmond for about five weeks to complete her therapy. It felt like we were packing her off for college. The hospital had an extended-stay floor, where patients, just like my mother, came to live during their treatment. It was dormitory-style living, and Momma met women from all over the state of Virginia, and from other states too, who had various forms of cancer they were battling. Part of her treatment included group meetings, where patients talked out their feelings of the illness to help them cope. I'm sure all this was of great benefit to my mother. I remember feeling lost and abandoned without her. She had never been away from us for such a lengthy time before, and I missed her terribly. Many more chores fell my way as the oldest, and a small seed of resentment planted itself inside me. I'm sure my father felt a tremendous amount of stress. I can relate to how he must have felt so well now that I am an adult with children of my own. But at the time, I just hated the direction that our lives were taking. I buried myself in schoolwork and the drama club. It felt so much better to convince myself that no matter how bad this cancer thing got, Momma would beat it, and she would get better. I had seen stories on TV and in magazines about how Pat Nixon had made a remarkable recovery from cancer. My mother could make a recovery like that too, I was sure. I decided that I would be the one to write a book detailing her recovery process, and it would be a best seller. Although I don't remember ever discussing the subject too deeply with my brothers at the time, they shared those feelings I had of things working out and Momma getting well again.

Toward the end of the summer, the cancer treatments ended, and my mother came home. There was a period of waiting to see if the radiation worked. I don't remember how long we waited, but the eventual result was that it hadn't gotten all of the cancer cells. The doctors suggested surgery. They would do a complete hysterectomy, and because the cancer had spread to her colon, part of that had to be removed, and a colostomy would be performed as well. This meant that Momma would have to wear a little bag to catch the waste leaving her body. My parents explained it all to the three of us. Momma would wear an elastic belt around her waist with the bag attached. Daddy would have to help her with changing it, kind of like when you change a baby's diaper, they said. I looked at my mother and tried to look supportive and hopeful. I couldn't let her know that all this sounded so awful to me. *How humiliating it must be for her*, I thought to myself. *It is so unfair. What did she ever do to deserve all this misery?* My strong relationship with God wouldn't allow me to place any blame on Him. It had to be the doctors. They hadn't done enough. *If something happens to my mother, it will be their fault*, I thought fiercely.

I hated going to MCV Hospital. It never seemed friendly to me. It didn't seem new enough or clean enough even though I knew it *had* to be clean to be a hospital. It was a large brick building several stories high located in a hilly part of downtown Richmond. It was difficult to find a parking space on the street. Often, Daddy had to circle the block several times to find an open space. We would put a bunch of change into the meter and then walk down the sidewalk to the hospital building. The sidewalks were cracked, and heat radiated up from them. The area seemed old and run-down. The entrance door to the hospital was small and unwelcoming. Just inside, the floor was made of old tiles, black and white diamonds, stretching down the narrow hallways. There were a lot of stairs, and the old lighting was dull and dim. It was quiet inside, and there was a scent in the air of pine mixed with rubbing alcohol. The oldness of the hospital made it seem unworthy, to me, of taking good care of my mother. Somehow in my mind, a newer hospital would take better care of my mother. No one greeted us or smiled at us, as I was used to them doing at Williamsburg Community Hospital. I remember feeling like we didn't belong there and wishing it was all a mistake. I didn't like the thought that my mother was in the hands of these people. It all seemed too foreign to me, not at all like home.

The first time we visited Momma at MCV was right after her hysterectomy. We used the elevator to get to her floor. It seemed like an eternity to me before we made it to Momma's room. It too had those black and white tiles. There wasn't much furniture besides the bed. The window was tall, almost to the ceiling, and made the room seem drafty even though I never felt a draft. It smelled better in there. It smelled like Momma. She'd had surgery two days ago and was still tired, but very happy to see us. We chatted awhile, and then Daddy took my brothers to get some snacks from a machine down the hall because they were getting restless. Momma said she wanted to show me something. She lifted up her hospital gown. I was hesitant about what I would see. She showed me the large incision across her abdomen. Large silver staples, spaced a quarter of an inch apart, closed the opening. The skin under the staples was pink with blotches of yellow from the iodine swabs. "It's like a great big smile wearing braces," she said, attempting humor. I laughed at her words, but inside I was horrified. Stapling a human being seemed so callous to me. I kept thinking how unbelievably brave my mother was to endure all this, from constant injections and IV needles, to this surgery, and now to be stapled! The recovery part was just beginning. The ordeal wasn't over yet by any means.

My parents never told us from the beginning that the doctors had suggested that my mother might have only had two years to live. I don't know how much they pushed to the back of their minds in order to cope and go on. But after the surgery, things seemed to take a slightly different turn. The doctors weren't able to remove all the cancerous tissue. They suggested a strong form of chemotherapy. It would be done on a rotating schedule of five-week periods. At the first of each month, Momma would go to Richmond for the day and receive the therapy as an outpatient. The doses of radiation made her so sick. She threw up the whole drive home. Then she would be sick in bed for two weeks or more because she was so weak. It was like she constantly had the flu. Finally, she would be feeling more like her old self again, and the fifth week would roll around, and she would go for another treatment. This horrible cycle went on for so long. My mother always seemed to be in bed. She talked about how she wanted things to be when she was gone. She seemed to have lost that fighting spirit. She wasn't as optimistic as she had been in the beginning. I listened intently and respectfully, but I hated to hear her speak of such a time. I would often respond to her, "We're just not going to let that happen." And I truly believed it wouldn't happen. Somehow, if we prayed hard enough, I thought, it just wouldn't happen. I felt so sure that God would send her a miracle. In my mind, God was a figure much like Santa Claus—a wise, loving, fatherly type who would not want any of his children to suffer.

When my brothers and I would argue, as typical siblings do, Momma would get so upset and say, "How can I leave this earth if you three can't get along? I'm counting on you to be there for each other, and your Daddy needs you also." I didn't like to think about that either, so maybe, just maybe, I argued with them sometimes because in my mind, it meant she couldn't go if we didn't get along perfectly.

I began to resent the pressure on me to help out all the time. I was a high school senior now and wanted to do things on my own time. I didn't mind doing things like dishes or laundry, but I wanted to do it in my time, not when my dad told me to. He didn't take too kindly to that attitude, and we had some whopper fights over the silliest of things. My brothers remember those yelling matches between our father and me better than I do, especially Richard, the more sensitive of the two. I hated all the changes in my mother. I could deal with the fact that she had lost most of her hair, and that she couldn't go to the bathroom like a normal person, but this illness had taken her spirit, her vim and vigor. I hated seeing her lying in bed, pale and weak, day after day. I wanted her to talk about when she got better instead of when she was gone. I didn't want her to be gone. I didn't like the way it made me feel, to think that she might have given up the fight. Somehow I thought if *I* was strong and tough, maybe it would help *her* to be that way too. Somehow, I had to be tough enough for both us.

My impending graduation from high school seemed to be something that brought a touch of Momma's sparkle back. I had applied and been accepted to Radford University. My mother had graduated from Radford and was secretly ecstatic that I chose that school. She never once tried to influence my decision in any way, and that must have made the fact that I chose her school even sweeter for her. She went on a quest for the perfect wig to make her look the way she would naturally. She didn't want to wear a scarf as she did around the house. She helped me make a list of whom to send graduation announcements to and pick out a pattern for a dress to make. She enjoyed looking over the newspaper advertisements to see where the bargains were for college-dormitory accessories. The main things I remember buying were a bright orange-and-yellow plaid blanket for my dorm bed and a big blue trunk. She said all college students needed a trunk. It wasn't often anymore that she felt like going out shopping, and that is why I remember that day so well. We had fun buying that big blue trunk together, just the two of us. She was determined to live long enough to see me graduate from high school.

I wish she could have had that same determination about getting better. But at the time, I took things as they came. I was so excited about the thought of going off to college and escaping the heavy burden of a dying mother, but I was very afraid too. I worried that something would happen if I left. I worried about a lot of unknowns. I just worried. I know that Momma sensed this. She had her own worries as strong as my own, but of a different origin. She worried that I would not go off and live my life if she died. She told me so often. "You must promise me," she said, "that you will go out and live your life, Elizabeth. Don't throw away good opportunities for the sake of this family." Then she would clarify it with "I mean, it is okay to be there for your brothers and your dad when they need you. Just don't sacrifice your happiness out of a sense of duty." But she had no need to clarify anything. I knew what she meant, and I think she knew that I would do what was best for everyone. Both my parents had instilled the importance of a college education in the three of us. Going to college seemed the most natural thing in the world to do; I couldn't imagine not going, much less not finishing. My parents had raised us to feel that college was the natural step after high school. My thoughts about going off to college were very idealistic, and romantic. I expected to treasure every minute of my time there, to make some very special and valuable friendships, and meet my future husband. I was determined that there would be no way I would give that up. I had grown up believing in "living happily ever after," so in my mind, everything had to work out. My mother had an incredible way of always making me feel empowered. I always felt like I could manage anything if I really wanted to do it. She really showed unconditional love.

My mother made it to my high school graduation. I know she and my dad were very proud of me that day. I was filled with so many emotions. It was very difficult for me to face being away from so many kids I had seen day in and day out over the last twelve years. Some classes of students are closer than others, and my high school class was one of the close-knit groups. I'm not fond of change. It is a scary thing for me most of the time. I am also a very sentimental and emotional person, so I cried a great deal that evening. Just about every picture of me taken that evening showed my splotchy red face. My mother was very concerned about me being so upset, but crying is a ritual for me that helps me cope and deal with changes and circumstances. I am so glad she was able to be there with me and share that day with me. I feel sad that my brothers never had the opportunity to have our mother at their own graduations too.

After my graduation, Momma's health declined a bit over the summer. The weather was hot and miserably humid. She stayed in bed a lot. But I was very busy. I had gotten a job as an interpreter at the silversmith shop in the restored area. It involved both telling the history of silversmithing and selling the silver jewelry in the shop next door. Best of all, I wore costumes, the traditional colonial attire for a middle-class young lady. It was a great summer job, and I made plenty of spending money for school. It gave me the independence I was craving. I liked knowing that I was a part of the "Colonial Williamsburg Foundation Family." Many teenagers wouldn't have liked being an extension of their father, but I didn't feel it overshadowed my identity. I liked being known as Dick Tisdale's daughter. I liked the challenge of consistently doing a good job and how that reflected well on our family. I liked the sense of security it brought me. Another benefit of the job was how busy I became. I had less time to worry about our family situation.

In mid-July, there was a weekend orientation at Radford for incoming freshmen. I was terribly excited and couldn't wait to get there. Before leaving Williamsburg, Daddy and I had to visit our bank. I was so naive, tagging along with my dad, so positive in my convictions that Daddy would take care of everything. When I had been in first grade, my parents had taken out some policy, which was supposed to build equity toward college tuition when I turned eighteen. My parents had been led to believe they had eight thousand dollars tucked away to help pay for my college tuition. But it had been some kind of scam because there was only eighty dollars. I know my parents must have been devastated. I was ready to go off to college, full of happy dreams of a fantastic future, and now they might not be able to afford to send me. But they never showed any of their worry or fear to me. Daddy had a friend at our bank to whom he had already told his dilemma. His friend suggested that I borrow the money needed to go to college from the state funds called the Virginia Education Loan Authority, or VELA program. I didn't know it then, but VELA was to become my best friend, financially speaking, over the course of the next five years. Even though my parents were disappointed about not being able to afford college for me, I was able to go anyway, and that had to have lifted their burden somewhat. I remember signing paper after paper, promising to repay the loans upon graduation. I did so with no reservation or worries. I really didn't understand fully the meaning of what I signed that day, but it was so far off in the future that I didn't give it a second thought. I only cared that I was able to go to college, and that my dreams were not disappointed.

Finally, we left for college orientation. My grandparents lived only fifteen minutes from campus, so we would be staying with them. Momma wasn't doing so well, and she wasn't able to attend all the student-parent meetings. Daddy and I were left to face the adventure together. I took charge of Daddy's wardrobe and chose what I wanted him to wear. Polo shirts with the alligator emblem were all the rage then. Daddy had a red one, a gift I had given him for his birthday. Naturally, I wanted to make a good impression on anyone we might meet on campus. That first day, he wore the red Izod shirt with a pair of navy-and-red-microchecked slacks that Momma had bought for him. I loved that outfit on him, and he looked so handsome in it, like he was ready for the golf course. Being color-blind, I don't know if my dad really realized how great he looked, but he loved seeing his "baby doll" happy. I remember walking around the campus arm in arm with him. He walked with a slight limp due to the prosthesis, but I never minded that. I was just so proud of him and happy to have him there with me. I felt tingly with excitement as we explored the campus together.

I signed up for classes that weekend and returned home with a feeling that nothing could rain on my parade. I knew in my heart that college was going to be the best experience of my lifetime. I had easily made friends that weekend and had felt none of the awkwardness I experienced in high school. I had felt poised and self-assured, and I really liked the way it felt. It was a chance for me to reinvent myself. When the end of August rolled around, I still felt the same way. My mother cried as they left me waving good-bye outside my dormitory. I didn't cry although there was a small lump in my throat. I was just so excited! My best childhood friend, Linda, was in the same dormitory as I. We had decided not to be roommates so we could meet other people and not rely on each other too much. She was upstairs, and I was down on the first floor. She had reservations about her roommate, Lauren. She was a tall redhead from Bedford, Virginia. Lauren was nice enough, but carried a lot of anger toward her parents. She was constantly complaining and was often pessimistic and negative. I had been given the delight of having two roommates due to overcrowding in the dorms. It was termed a triple and was, in the majority of cases, destined for disaster.

Anytime you put three females together, two will pair off, and one will be left out. Rayann was my designated roommate. She was from Roanoke and was a very sweet girl. She also had a best friend on campus who was a sophomore. Rayann spent a lot of time with her sophomore friend.

Our third roommate was a very forward and self-assured young lady named Leslie. She was from Northern Virginia, or NOVA as she called it. She enjoyed taking charge. I have never done well with headstrong types who want to be in charge of everything. Even with my newfound self-confidence, I didn't enjoy dealing with Leslie's strong personality, so I got into the habit of spending a lot of time up in Linda's room instead of in my own. But doing that allowed Rayann and Leslie to become closer, and they ended up doing a lot of things together simply because I wasn't around. Linda, in turn, was not endearing herself to her own roommate. She was getting very tired of hearing Lauren complain about everything all the time. By the time October came, we both were very upset about our rooming situation. De-tripling was supposed to take place by November 1, which meant Leslie would finally be out of my room. The problem was that Rayann had decided she really wanted to move in with her best friend, the sophomore, in another building. Leslie had ideas of her own. Unaware of Rayann's feelings, Leslie wanted me to move out so she and Rayann could be roommates. I just wanted both of them to move out so Linda and I could be roommates and Linda could get away from Lauren. In the end, I finally got my wish, but not without a lot of prior drama!

CHAPTER FOUR

My high school had homecoming on the first weekend in October. It was very important to both Linda and me to go. We found a ride going to Williamsburg and made plans to attend several parties, as well as the football game. I was especially looking forward to all the activities because as a high school student, I never attended many parties or football games because I had to help out at home. My mother was very happy to have me home, more so than I realized at the time. Looking back, I think she must have used that visit as a benchmark. She had been worried about my adjusting to college. With the roommate situation, I had made a couple tearful phone calls home, and I think she wasn't sure what to expect. But there I was, Miss Social Butterfly, attending parties and appearing to have no care in the world. This was such a different role for me, for I usually would stay at home to help out. Maybe that was the sign she needed, that at last her worries could be put to rest. Maybe it showed her I was growing up and could handle having to take charge if things took a turn for the worse. I didn't realize it then, but Momma wasn't doing well. Maybe a part of me did realize it, but I wouldn't face up to it. Otherwise, I would have canceled those party plans and spent as much time with my mom as possible. I remember sitting on her bed with her talking girl talk about classes and friends. She filled me in about her treatments and such. I remember so distinctly sighing and saying, "It doesn't look like you'll ever get better," and hugging her. I still regret those words today. They haunt me often as I can hear myself saying them over and over in my mind. I often wonder, if I had never said that to her, maybe she wouldn't have given up and kept fighting that cancer battle? My saying that to her must have allowed her to think I had accepted her not getting well. But I really didn't. I just said it without thinking, more as a reaction to her tales of treatment and medication. I will never know for sure. And under the circumstances, she probably could have never won that battle anyway. The odds against her were so great.

Parents' Weekend came to Radford on the last weekend of October. I was disappointed that my own parents were unable to come, and I had a lonely and left-out feeling as I watched other students greeting their parents. The day was gray and drizzly. It seemed to match my mood as I watched happy students greeting even happier parents in the parking lot outside my window. Leslie's parents arrived, showering her with presents and affection. Her mother made over me in an artificial sort of way. At one point, she said one of my pet peeve comments. "What a pretty face you have." Her tone sounded genuine, but I knew her comment really meant she thought I should loose a few pounds. I certainly didn't look at all like Leslie—tall, thin, athletic, and blonde. I could only imagine the kinds of things Leslie had told them about me. It was no secret that we were not especially fond of each other. And I had not opened up much to Leslie about my mother's situation. I had told Rayann some of it, but mostly, I kept the details to myself. Linda was the only one who knew the depth of it all.

Linda's mother was due to arrive soon, and she was as close to a parent as I could get for the weekend. I had known Mrs. Bland since I was about three, and her son, Carlyle, was my brother Richard's very closest friend. You never saw one without the other, and usually Donald tagged along behind them. I didn't know until later, but her trip to see Linda and me was twofold. Momma's health was declining quickly, and Mrs. Bland had come to take me home. Linda and I went from being so excited to see her mother to feeling a grave urgency to pack quickly and be on our way home. That wonderful feeling of being safe in that campus world melted away. The past was catching up with me again; I couldn't escape it. Mrs. Bland said that my mother might not make it through the night. How had that happened? I wondered to myself. I had just talked to her a day ago, and she seemed the same. Not great, but not this bad.

I don't remember much about packing up, just a panicked rush to throw a few outfits into a suitcase and hoping it would be enough to get me through a long weekend. I don't remember if I told Rayann or Leslie good-bye or why I was leaving. I don't remember if I told anyone at all. I mostly remember being in the car heading for home and wishing the trip was shorter than five hours. It would be ten o'clock at night before we would get there. I watched the mountain scenery whiz by, blurry, as I was lost in thought. It became dark before we reached Richmond. I knew this part of the highway so well. We were getting closer, but still not close enough. My stomach churned with anticipation. I felt such a sense of urgency, but at the same time, I tried to ignore the reasons why I felt that way. They were too terrible to acknowledge. When we exited the interstate, the excited feeling in the pit of my stomach grew. It wasn't a happy excitement, more an anxious feeling about the unknown mixed with a gladness about being home. *Home, home . . . almost home . . .* The little tune frolicked through my mind. The anticipation was stronger than I'd ever felt. The ten-minute drive from the exit ramp seemed an eternity. Finally, we rounded the corner. Home was in sight. There were a couple of cars in the driveway. It looked like every light was on in the house. The back of my neck tingled. My head felt like little fireworks were going off inside, and each one screamed "No no, something is wrong!" as it exploded. And something definitely wasn't right. My parents never would have allowed so many lights to be left on at one time. Why were there guests at my house so late at night? I think I remember someone voicing the very fears I was thinking, Linda's mother perhaps. "Something's up!" I have no recollection of getting out of the car, or whether someone greeted me at the door. Just suddenly, Daddy was there with the saddest face I had ever seen him wear. I knew what he was going to say even before he said it, and I'll never forget his words. "Your mother's gone," he said in almost a whisper. My heart felt like it had stopped. Everything stopped—the air, time itself. The living room where we stood dissolved into emptiness. Nothing moved except Daddy's lips. "She died about an hour ago," he continued. "Her poor, tired body just couldn't go on anymore. There was too much fluid in her lungs." Daddy sat down on the loveseat. It took a lot of effort for him to continue talking. He looked so tired and drained. I didn't want to hear the reality of what he was saying, and yet I was mesmerized by his every word. I couldn't tear my eyes away from his face.

"I was in the room with her holding her hand until the last." His voice wavered a bit, but he kept talking. "I knew when her spirit left her body. I could feel a caring, warm presence envelope the room. I didn't say good-bye. I kissed her hand and said until we meet again." Silent tears rolled down his cheeks. It was almost more than I could bear to see my father in the pits of despair and know that my mother was gone. It was the most tragic, gut-wrenching sight I ever witnessed.

He broke down totally, and some family friend took him off to comfort him. There was such a burning lump in my throat. It hurt so much, all the way down deep into my chest. I stood there in shock for a moment, and then my surroundings seemed real again. I turned on my heel and hurried down the hallway back to my own bedroom, half blinded by hot tears as they filled my eyes. My room looked the same as when I had left it only a few weeks before, only it felt different now. Momma was gone. Every corner of the room seemed to scream the awful truth. *She's gone, she's gone!* Even the house felt sad. I closed the bedroom door and stood there for a moment, trying to fight back the tears. Suddenly, out of that incredible sadness came an overwhelming rage. The heat of it coursed through my veins and overtook me from head to toe like an enraged dragon. Why hadn't Momma waited for me to arrive at her side? I had missed seeing her by an hour . . . one lousy hour! She owed me a good-bye. It wasn't fair. It just wasn't fair. Tears were streaming down my face. I was no longer able to keep them at bay. I was so angry, but I felt guilty about feeling angry. And I felt so sad. My life was changed forever, and I would never have it back again as it was, never.

I have a letter today that I cherish very much. It is from my dear friend and once minister, Rev. George Tompkins. He sent me the letter after I told him I was writing this book. It is a personal account of the last hours of my mother's life, and I feel that he tells it so much better than I ever could.

I went back to the hospital after supper. I think your mother had already slipped into a deep sleep. I don't remember there being any pain or anxiety on her part, but I felt totally helpless in some ways. I guess we all knew that we were at the end, but your father seemed so low—no one ever wants to give up hope, and I think he wanted to cling to some hope, but we were losing her. I guess we just sort of visited for a long time. Sometimes we didn't speak at all, which can be sort of nice. Dr. Brown came in to check on your mother around eight o'clock or so. When he was finished, your father said with such sadness that I remember his exact words, "I don't think she's going to make it through the night." Dr. Brown (I guess unthinkingly) said, "I don't think she's going to make it through the next fifteen minutes." That's when I wanted to hit him, but maybe it was good, because it made your father and me realize that the worst, in some ways was over. Again, she was peaceful and no longer speaking, and he sat in a chair right next to her bed, holding her hand. The nurses, who were wonderful, kept checking in, and I can't quite remember if her nurse at some point just decided to stay in the room or that I went and got the nurse. Almost imperceptibly, your mother just slipped away. I don't think in those days they had people hooked up on those monitors that show oxygen level, pulse, and blood pressure—I hate them because a family can see the numbers getting lower and lower. For your mother, it could not have been any better or easier. I can imagine her simply falling asleep in this world and waking up just as peaceful in the next, but healed and whole and happy. If I could paint, though, I could still do a picture of your father's face—it is an image of grief I'll always carry. His emotions were gentle, nothing melodramatic. I remember standing behind him and rubbing his shoulder. I think he kissed her hand, and again I had one of those painful moments. I could see his tears left on her hand. It was touching and powerful all at once. I think we had been reading some psalms and had done the litany for the dying. We said the commendatory prayers from the prayer book. Then after a short while, he had to deal with the practicalities that unfortunately always accompany a death. In some ways, holding his arm and leaving the room seemed far more agonizing than her death. It's the feeling not really of loss only but also of knowing our world goes on . . . but differently . . . and with an emptiness for him that I do not know was ever filled again. This sounds contradictory, but it's almost encouraging in such a moment to see the pain of love.

Sometime the following day, the clergy from Bruton Parish came to visit us. I remember Dr. Lewis, head minister, cupping my face by the chin as he spoke to me. He had a reputation for being larger than life, stubborn, and overbearing at times; however, he did genuinely care about his parishioners. His face was too close to mine; and his teeth, yellowed with age, were gritted into a forced grin. My ears couldn't believe the words he spoke. "We all know she has paid a dear price for not going to the doctor earlier," he was saying. My face remained unchanged, half smiling as he spoke. But did he notice the fire flash in my eyes? *It is a good thing he can't read my mind,* I thought. *He was supposed to be here to comfort our family. How dare he say anything against my mother! She is dead. She doesn't deserve anyone's criticism.*

When he finished passing on his advice and comments about my mother to me, he uncupped my chin and moved on to one of my brothers. Deep down, I knew his intentions were good, but I was indignant and hurt by his choice of words. I was unable to accept my mother having any blame for what had happened to her. The associate minister, Rev. George Tompkins, came up to me next. I adored him. He remains one of the kindest individuals I have ever known. I had turned to him for help and advice on several occasions during my mother's illness. He always knew what to say to make me feel better. He seemed to understand an awkward teenager's feelings. He took me aside to talk. Perhaps he had seen that flash of defiance in my eyes when Dr. Lewis had spoken to me. "I stayed with your mother a good part of the day yesterday, Elizabeth," he said in his soothing, soft-spoken manner. "She wasn't the person you remember at the end. She was so zapped of her strength. It would have been too painful for you to have seen her that way." I interrupted him, protesting quietly, "But I wanted to say good-bye! I should have been able to say good-bye." He understood my pain, but it didn't change his advice. "I know you feel that way, but I was there. It wouldn't have been good for you to be there. God has a plan in mind, and things happen the way they do for a reason. You may not agree with that plan, but it is probably for the best."

George Tompkins meant well, I knew that. He had been there with my mother and had seen how it was. I knew what he was saying was probably right, and yet I couldn't help but envy him for having been there when I could not. I didn't argue with him anymore. But I didn't change my mind either, at least not for a long time. I regret very deeply to this day that I never got to say good-bye to my mother as she slipped away from us into that unknown world of heaven that long-ago night in October. But now years later, since having read that letter from George Tompkins, I accept that he truly was right all along. I'm glad that I didn't intrude on that private moment between my parents. It was meant to be theirs alone, and I accept God's wisdom for that.

The day of my mother's funeral was one of the most gorgeous days I can ever remember. The sky was the bluest possible, with only a few white trailing clouds. The air was cool, with a bite to it, but the bright sunshine warmed you just enough to make you feel comfortable. Momma loved the fall. She would have said the air was "crisp like a fresh apple." I felt like she had specially ordered it just so we would know she was okay, wherever she was. The previous two days had been draining on everyone. I had helped my dad make all the arrangements from choosing music for the service to picking out the casket. I remember parts of the trip to the funeral home. Daddy wanted the perfect casket without it being too expensive and overly fussy. Apparently, he and my mother had discussed her funeral arrangements before her death, and she had made him promise not to spend too much. But he had always wanted to give her the best that he could, and that had not changed just because she died. Perhaps that is why I remember picking out the casket with him. The room was filled with caskets of all kinds. I especially remember one that was powder blue with a beautiful quilted white satin lining. Many were various shades of beige; some were darker colors like navy blue or wine red. Daddy wanted wood—real wood because he felt it suited Momma more.

Real wood caskets were much more expensive than the metal ones. I recall thinking that was so strange because it used to be that everyone was buried in a plain pine box. We ended up choosing a metal one that was painted to look like wood. Inside, it was lined with white satin and had a white satin pillow for Momma's head. That was a feature important to me. And Daddy got the kind that would be sealed inside a kind of vault, which was guaranteed to not leak or rot for twenty-five years or more. I thought that was strange too because when one is dead, it doesn't matter if your casket is waterproof. But it made Daddy feel better, and that was most important to me. He had lost his life partner, and I wanted him to find some kind of happiness, no matter how small.

The evening before the funeral was a visitation evening at the funeral parlor. I wore an outfit that I had made for college and that Momma had loved on me. It was a rose-colored skirt and vest with a striped blouse of various shades of rose, pink, and burgundy. I felt confident in the outfit, and I knew I needed to feel good about myself in order to face all those people with a smile. The four of us were rather somber when we arrived. The place was too quiet even though soft music played in the background. There was a feeling in the air, a kind of heaviness. We all knew none of us wanted to be there, but we all felt we had to be there. Richard and Donald kind of just followed me around without talking too much. That was so unlike us. We usually were full of energy when we were together—telling jokes, teasing each other, and laughing. Some friends of the family were already there. I especially remember two of my parents' best friends, Kaye and Wallace Robertson, being there. They are two of the kindest, most comforting people I have ever known. I wandered about the main room of the funeral home. The garnet-colored carpet hushed my footsteps. There was a book for guests to sign, sitting on a stand beside the entrance to another room. The lighting was more muted inside there. I didn't realize it was a viewing room. I was just looking around, noticing the people who were visiting. I wandered inside the room. Wallace and Kaye were talking to another couple. Kaye was facing me, and she smiled over at me warmly. I returned her smile, and as I glanced away, that's when I noticed the casket.

Even though I knew Momma was gone, I wasn't prepared for the shock that hit me like a ton of bricks when I saw my mother's still form lying in that casket. The realization of her death hit me with such force as though I had been physically punched. I had been playing a game of being strong and not really facing up to the truth. But there she was, lying in a casket, and I couldn't hide from the truth anymore. I had a surge of conflicting emotions. I felt an overwhelming urge to run over to her and shake her to wake her up. And a stronger feeling was to run out of the room, screaming at the top of my lungs until I awoke from this horrible dream. But I couldn't do either. I just stood there as though my feet were bolted to the floor, trying to fight back a rush of tears. Momma just looked like she was asleep, as I had seen her so many times before. But another part of me knew she was dead, and that here was this lifeless figure who looked like my mother, but had no life left in it anymore. I was afraid of that part of my mother. I could no longer hold back the sobs. I had to turn away, and Kaye Robertson hugged me and helped me compose myself.

A while later, I got up the courage to go closer to the casket. I had only seen two dead bodies in my life. One when I was very young, about four years old. She had been my father's aunt, Julia, and I had not really known her. My mother had been unable to attend her funeral because Richard had been a small baby, so I had attended the funeral with my dad. I have a gauzy memory of a woman with very red lips, who looked like a wax doll lying in a casket. The other was more recently. Five years before, my dear Aunt Bettie had died from complications stemming from her long illness of multiple sclerosis. She too had seemed pale and waxy as I had looked at her in her casket. I had not been afraid of looking at her, only of touching her. I remember seeing many people, including my own mother, come up and touch Aunt Bettie's hand. I couldn't bring myself to do that then, and now, looking down on my own mother, I couldn't touch her either. I wanted to so badly, but I just couldn't make my hand reach out. I had these wild visions in my mind of her eyes flashing open suddenly as I touched her and looking like a demon or something. I felt incredibly guilty and ashamed of myself for having those silly thoughts about my own mother. I just stood there, looking down at her. She was wearing the long yellow dress she had made to wear to a twenty-fifth high school reunion formal party a few years earlier. I always thought she looked very pretty in that dress. Around her neck was her favorite seed pearl rope necklace. She was wearing her wedding and engagement rings, and I stared at them hard, wishing

I could reach out and touch that soft hand. But I was so afraid of it feeling cold and lifeless.

Kaye Robertson walked over to me again as I stood there. She touched my mother's hand, patting it. I noticed for the first time there was makeup on the hand to cover up the bruising made by IV needles. I felt a twinge of envy at seeing her hold Momma's hand. "She looks good," Kaye said, her face looking so very sad. "At least she is not in any pain anymore." "Yes," I answered her, almost in a whisper. "They aren't planning to bury her in her rings, are they?" she asked me. "No," I answered. "They will go to Richard and Donald after tonight. "Will you save the necklace for yourself?" she asked. I shook my head no. "She should wear it," I answered. "It goes with the dress, and I want it to be with her." Kaye nodded and hugged me again. I don't remember much else about that evening, only that it was difficult, and exhausting.

All the hardships of those last two days faded into the blueness of a beautiful sky that morning. Momma would have called it sweater weather, and that is exactly what I decided to wear to her funeral. I hadn't brought a great deal of clothes home with me from college. I had to rely on what was left in my closet at home and hadn't been taken to college to begin with. I chose an olive-green-and-cream-patterned cardigan sweater with a plain tan wool shirt. I was determined not to wear black. I felt better wearing something my mother had liked on me. I didn't care what anyone else thought. It only mattered that I do what I thought was right.

The service itself remains a bit sketchy in my mind. I remember being very moved by the music. We had taken great pains to go through the hymnal and choose songs that had been my mother's favorites. She had loved so many that it had not been an easy task. My brothers and I focused on one song in particular that she taught us when we were small. "All Things Bright and Beautiful" seemed to sum up her feelings about God and the world. The three of us cannot hear that song to this day without thinking of our mother.

I remember Daddy was able to be fairly composed. And I remember that the church seemed so stark and somber. I remember thinking it should have been adorned with flowers everywhere to show her love of nature and that her life had been so beautiful and important and vivid. The solemnness seemed to take away from that. I was told that this is how Episcopal funeral services are done. That is the first time I remember questioning Episcopal practices and wishing some of the rules and customs were different.

My Uncle Don spoke at Momma's funeral. He has a beautiful speaking voice. I have always been amazed at his composure. He spoke at Aunt Bettie's funeral too, and his voice never wavered once. I knew that to maintain such composure must take mountains of strength. Now here again, he was speaking about a sister at her funeral, only this sister was his own twin. They had been so close, yet he spoke with a clear, steady voice. I could break down at the mere thought of my mother and what she had been through. I wondered how it was possible for him not to cry. *God must surely be holding his hand*, I thought.

My mind strayed to thoughts of all my mother had been to me. This church had been such a center of her life. I thought about what she looked like all dressed for church. That great smell of cosmetics mixed with her perfume. She only wore Charisma made by Avon, and she usually wore the same color red lipstick; Mulled Wine, it was called. She always looked beautiful to me, but most especially when she was dressed up. I loved her black coat with the real mink collar and the way its fur framed her face. Sitting there with my eyes closed, I could almost smell her perfume and see her smiling at me in her loving way. I wanted desperately to be able to open my eyes and see her sitting next to me. When we left the church after the service, I remember following behind the casket as it was lowered down the steps to the hearse. I stepped out of the shaded light of the church and into the bright sunshine in a vivid blue sky. A playful wind whipped by, twirling some golden fall leaves as they blew past. It was as though my Momma's spirit was right next to me, letting me know things would be all right, and I could find joy in all this if I looked carefully.

My mother was to be buried in Sunset Cemetery in Christiansburg, the town where she grew up. After the funeral in Williamsburg, the whole family packed up and headed for the mountains and my grandparents' house. I knew we would be swamped with old family friends visiting at the house. Each would bring a delicious dish of something good to eat, a Southern tradition I had become used to in the last few years. The thought of all that company made me feel better. Nothing could make you feel happier than the warmth of a close family, except maybe Momma's warm arms around me, and that just wasn't possible anymore.

The day we buried my mother was a bit grayer than before, but the view of the mountains from the top of Sunset Cemetery was beautiful. The old family burial plot was full. Momma and Daddy had purchased plots in a newer section closer to the top of the hill. The family plot had only one spot left, and it was for my Uncle B. I remember that day he showed us his burial spot. It was right next to the road, and he said that cars driving past would be keeping him awake for all eternity. Richard and Donald and I laughed so much over this comment that day, and I still get a chuckle about it when I remember him saying it. We needed a bit of humor that day, and he was our best medicine.

CHAPTER FIVE

I returned to college after the weekend was over. It was almost like returning from another planet. The surroundings were familiar, but I felt so different. I had missed Halloween, which was supposed to be a big event on campus. That seemed strange to me. Halloween was one of our family's favorite celebrations. Daddy loved to wear a scary mask and answer the door for trick-or-treaters. Momma always made her special owl cookies. And my brothers and I always decorated our yard. It was a holiday we had enjoyed so much year after year, and yet this year, I had not even thought about Halloween once. Now it was over. We were already one week into November, and everyone was thinking about Thanksgiving holidays. The girls on the floor of my dormitory had gotten together and bought me a plant. I remember reading the sympathy card. It was the first time the reality of what I had been through hit home to me in the world outside my own family. I felt so different now from all the other girls who had mothers to call home to. I would never be able to celebrate Mother's Day again. No more mother-daughter talks or shopping sprees together at the mall. I felt strange when I walked past the pay telephone booth on my dormitory floor.

Not so long ago, I had talked to my mother on that very phone. It was our last communication together. We had talked about how my classes were going and how I was trying to make the best of my triple-roommate situation. She had sounded weak, but cheerful, and as usual, encouraging. I had never detected a sign of how bad her condition was becoming. I had no inkling that I might never hear her voice again after that phone call. Now I felt like that phone booth may as well have had a sign saying For Mother-Daughter Calls Only. Would I be able to handle this new life without my mother? I had promised her that I would, and more than that, my dad and my brothers needed me to handle it. No, not just handle it, but really go on with life and be there for them. I could set a good example, I thought. One that Momma would be proud of. And so I tried my best.

It wasn't easy though. I had missed almost a week of classes, and I had to go to each of my professors and explain what had happened. All of them were very understanding and helpful, except my math teacher. Math was not my best subject, so I wasn't doing extremely well in the class anyway. I'd missed a test while I was gone, and my teacher wasn't too happy about that. He told me it was too bad about my mother, but that was life, and I needed to deal with it. He wouldn't let me make up for the test. When I told my Uncle B. about it, he was furious. But there really was nobody who could do anything about it, except me. I studied as best as I could. Studying wasn't so easy. I would often drift off into thought, remembering different times and thinking about Momma. Looking back, I realize I was not allowing myself enough time to digest all that had happened to me. Failure at something was impending. I failed the math class. When I arrived home from the first quarter, I jokingly told Daddy that my grades were a reflection of my entire future at the university. I had earned a representative of each grade available to students! The A was in history of drama. The B was in freshman English. The C was in American history. The D was in sociology, and the F was, of course, math. "This," I told my dad, "represents all you can expect from me in college. I just hope to see more of the As, Bs, and Cs, and less of those other two." I joked. "Me too," he agreed and then added, "but I'll be proud of you no matter what." Daddy never pressured me over grades. He was just proud of me for going to college, period. I eventually would perform much better in school; I just had to get used to the way my new life would be.

When I came home for Christmas just two months after Momma's death, I knew it would be a challenge to make it a happy holiday for our family. I met that challenge head-on, determined that it would be special. Christmas has always been a magical time for my family. It was Daddy's favorite time of year, but naturally, this year, he didn't seem so happy. I decided it was best not to do everything the way we had done so in the past. Traditionally, we put up the tree in our family room beside the fireplace. Since I had been about ten, we used an artificial tree. The year before, Momma had suddenly wanted a real tree, and we had bought the biggest one that would fit in the room. I think she suspected that it might have been her last Christmas. I decided that we shouldn't go to such expense again this year. My brothers and I put together the artificial tree and set it up in the living room instead of in the family room. It was a welcome change for my dad, and I began to see some of the old sparkle once again in his eyes. He had lost a lot of weight and seemed so frail. He wore his bathrobe a lot, claiming that he was cold. I decided to get him an electric blanket as a Christmas present. I knew he must feel lost in that big bed all alone without the warm body of his wife beside him like he had been used to for the last twenty-one years. Richard and Donald had found a bargain at the local hobby store on some train cars and accessories for Dad's electric train set. That hobby consumed him now. Dad often could be found up in the attic where his world of trains was located. My brothers and I were certain that we had the makings for a great Christmas despite the loss we were trying to forget.

I remember it as a pretty good Christmas too. I tried so hard to act as though everything was great. I was becoming the glue that held the family together. I didn't mind then; I still don't mind today. It is my lot in life in many ways, and I am happy to fill that spot. It is a wondrous feeling to be needed so much. We took a lot of pictures that Christmas. Daddy looks so worn and weathered when I look at them, but my brothers and I are full of smiles and laughter. I am glad of that because I know that Daddy needed to see us happy. I didn't realize it then, but he was finding it harder and harder to go on as normal. His body was under a lot of stress anyway from the diabetes. He was inching slowly downhill, and I don't know if he himself even realized it.

I finished up the first year of college without any major problems. I took the math course again and passed. I was anxious to get back home for the summer and help out. I knew Daddy missed me desperately; I could hear it in his voice when we talked on the phone. Daddy and my brothers made the trip to pick me up from college. Daddy was surprised when he saw all the extra things I had accumulated. "You're taking a lot more home than you brought with you in the fall," he remarked. We spent the weekend with my grandparents before returning home. I left some of my college things that I wouldn't need over the summer with them.

Once I was home, I took charge right away with planning and cooking meals, cleaning up, and making a few decorative changes to the house. There were too many reminders of Momma about, and I thought a new rug and curtains might do the trick. I returned to my summer job with Colonial Williamsburg at the silversmith shop. I especially enjoyed being able to go to services at Bruton Parish Church again. My brothers enjoyed having a female's touch about the house. Someone else to clean and cook the meals and help care for them comforted them a great deal. Everything seemed great. It was at this time I first noticed the dove. She had made a nest in one of the pine trees growing in our side yard. She was a light gray color—a mourning dove, I was told. I had never known of doves nesting in neighborhood yards the way robins or cardinals do. I thought doves were rarer than that. Her nest was on a lower branch, about eye level to me. I spotted her when I was carrying some garbage out to the trashcans one day. I scarcely dared to breathe as I watched her. I was less than two feet away from the nest. The dove eyed me cautiously but never moved off her nest or ruffled her feathers. She seemed to sense that I wouldn't harm her. I took it as a sign. Perhaps Momma was watching over us in the form of this dove! I was comforted by the sound of the dove's cooing each morning. I came to count on hearing it each day. Then I began to notice hearing it when I was feeling sad or frustrated. Curiously, I always seemed to hear the dove's cooing at just those times when I needed spiritual reassurance. I didn't know it then, but the dove would come to be a special sign for me as I grew older and continued on with my life.

On July 8, we received a surprising and unexpected phone call. My Uncle Don called to tell us that my grandfather had died suddenly of heart failure. He was almost ninety-one years old, so he had lived a great, long life. But considering all that we had just been through six months before with my mother, it came as a great shock to all of us, especially me. With the college campus so close to my grandparents' home, I had spent many weekends visiting with them. I think that spending time with them helped me with the healing process after my mother died. My brothers seemed numbed by the news. My father was very troubled by it, and I could tell he was afraid of dealing with the trauma of another funeral so soon after Momma's. He used work as an excuse not to go to the funeral in Christiansburg. He had missed so much work already this year in dealing with my mother's illness; it really wasn't an excuse at all. But it allowed his conscience to be clear and got him out of putting himself in a dreaded situation. I don't know how the rest of my family feels about us missing my grandfather's funeral, but I am glad. I have the best memories of him, and they are not clouded by visions of him lying in a casket. I remember him with laughter, smiles, and vitality. Funerals seem to take some of that away, at least to me they seem to. My grandmother didn't take the loss of her husband well at all. They had been married for over sixty years, and she was devastated by his death. Not long after his funeral, she fell in the bathroom and broke her hip. She had to spend a lot of time in a convalescent hospital after her fall and eventually had to move in and live with my Uncle Don and his family in Suffolk, Virginia.

It seemed like things couldn't get any worse in our family, but they did one Saturday afternoon, about a month after my grandfather's death. I had been shopping to pick up some groceries. I pulled into the driveway and prepared to unload them when Donald came flying out of the front door of the house. "Daddy is talking funny!" he told me in an excited panic. "He can't seem to remember what his own name is or what my name is." Those words brought fear to my heart. I wasn't sure what was wrong, but I knew it was not good. Daddy wandered over to the door before I had a chance to go into the house. He had a most puzzled expression on his face. He was mumbling to himself. He pointed to me. "And you," he said, "you are important to me. You—" I interrupted him. "It's me, Daddy . . . Elizabeth, your daughter." He still seemed puzzled, but he smiled as though my words had reassured him. Then he went on. "I can't remember what the name of that thing is," he said, gesturing up toward the attic where his train set was located. He kept describing it and trying to figure it out. It felt like the world was crashing all around me, but I fought back the urge to break down under its weight. The back of my neck was tense, and I felt lightheaded.

I questioned Donald about what had happened. He couldn't tell me much. Just that Daddy had been fine one minute, and then the next, he seemed out of it. I called the neighbors where Richard was playing and told him to come straight home. I got everyone into the car and drove to the emergency room. It turned out that Daddy had suffered a small stroke. It was a very minor one as strokes go, they told us, but it had been traumatic enough for me. Daddy stayed in the hospital for about a week. He suffered from a severe headache for days. He told me that nothing they gave him brought him any relief. At the time, I had little use for doctors. Who could blame me? In my eyes, they had just allowed my mother to die. I remember taking the belt from my dad's robe and tying it around his head tightly. That was a trick Momma had taught me for relieving a bad headache. Daddy said it made him feel better. That was all I cared about. The nurses looked at me like I was silly, but I didn't care as long as Daddy felt better. By the end of the summer, Daddy was pretty much himself again.

The only lasting effect he suffered from the stroke was an inability to concentrate when trying to read. He told me that the words seemed to float all over the page, and he would get headaches if he tried to read for too long. That was quite a loss for him because after losing my mother, reading had been something he enjoyed, and it took his mind off my mother's absence. It seemed like he couldn't catch a break, I thought to myself. Daddy ended up devoting even more time to his train set in the attic. I was so glad that he had that outlet. He went on part-time disability from work and only worked a partial week. The doctors felt he needed to relax more and reduce his stress. I guess my returning to college added to his stress, though he never let on about that at all. He always made me feel so special, and I knew he was so proud of me for going. He and I were becoming even closer as time passed after my mother's death. I imagine that he felt comforted by being with me because I was a lot like my mother. He enjoyed talking about her to me and speculating how she might have reacted to things that were happening to us. He told me that she had asked him to promise that he would consider remarrying if the opportunity ever presented itself. Daddy said that he couldn't imagine being married to anyone else but her. He had attended a few lunches with some women friends but hadn't really enjoyed himself, he said. No one could compare to my mother in his eyes. Some of the other women had seemed silly and shallow, too giggly, he said.

He made it through another school year uneventfully. I'm sure it took great strength of both mind and body to make it through those nine months until I returned home again for the summer. This second summer started off quietly. Again, I returned to my summer job at Colonial Williamsburg as an interpreter. As in the previous summer, I fell into the routine of cooking and cleaning and shopping and caring for everyone, as my mother had before me. Not long into the summer, however, Daddy ended up suffering a mild heart attack. I don't recall many of the details of how it happened. I remember visiting him in the ICU and seeing the wires hooked up to him. I remember the doctors telling me that it had only been a mild heart attack, and that there had been little damage. They also speculated that his body was worn down by the diabetes, and his emotional state, since Momma's death, wasn't helping. He spent a couple weeks in the hospital and then came home again. I spent the rest of the summer caring for him, helping him to regain his strength, and reducing his stress as much as I knew how. I don't know how I pulled everyone through those times. When I think about it today, I feel so overwhelmed by the fact that I handled things as well as I did. I know my youth was on my side. A lack of wisdom can give you a determination that is harder to find after you've experienced life a bit more. When you are naive, you don't know how to give up. But my Daddy fought back as well, with a strength not to be found in most people. He defied all the doctors; and once again, by the end of the summer, he was back to his usual self, and I set off again to start my junior year in college.

My junior year turned out to be my very best year academically. I made the dean's list with straight As after the winter quarter. I remember being home on holiday and just screaming with excitement when the mail arrived and I saw my grades. Daddy was so proud of me. The winter was a hard one that year. There was a lot of snow.

I didn't know about it at the time, but later on, my brothers related a tale to me of how they all three got stuck in the snow while on a mission to get heating oil. Daddy had allowed the furnace to run out, and they were driving to get an emergency refill to hold them until the truck could make a delivery. Daddy must have been under a tremendous amount of stress, but he never let on to me. Our telephone conversations were always upbeat and happy. But all that he dealt with during the year would catch up to him by the time summer would roll around. A pattern began to emerge. When I returned home for the summer this time, I anticipated some kind of medical problem to occur. It had happened for the last two summers, so I was on my guard. At first, things seemed like they would remain uneventful. We were experiencing a lot of difficulties with our car. I was worried that I would not be able to rely on it when I needed to. It quit on me in the middle of an intersection on a rainy day one afternoon, and it was then I decided we needed to purchase a new vehicle. A family friend recommended a dealer friend of hers who was sympathetic to our situation.

The salesman was most helpful in getting us a good deal on a slightly used car at a very reasonable price. We brought home a cream-colored Chevrolet Citation. But it wasn't long after this purchase that Daddy's kidneys began to fail. It was just at the time of my twenty-first birthday, because I remember the disappointment of having to celebrate such a special event without my father. He was taken to Williamsburg Community Hospital, where after only a few days, his doctors told me they wanted to move him. They said he needed care that their hospital wasn't able to provide. They suggested moving him to Norfolk, where there was a hospital specializing in severe kidney problems. I was overwhelmed. How could I work, run a household, and visit my dad every day if he was fifty miles away? Help came from Bruton Parish Church. George Tompkins had since moved on to another parish, but the other associate helping Dr. Lewis, named Sam Portaro, was just as wonderful to us. Both Sam and the organist at our church, James S. Darling, took time out of their busy schedules to teach me the route from Williamsburg to the hospital in Norfolk. Often they would drive with us, or even go on their own just to visit my father and see how he was doing. The doctors in Norfolk, who didn't know much of my father's history other than his medical one, weren't overly optimistic about his recovery. They didn't think he would live out the summer. And everyone tried to prepare the three of us for the impending departure of another parent. Somehow, it all didn't seem real to me. I couldn't see myself saying good-bye to my dad yet. We needed him so badly. Richard and Donald had grown an especially strong bond with him. They were overly protective of him and put him on a pedestal. It seemed that my father felt too that it wasn't his time. As the summer wore on, he made what the doctors called a miraculous recovery. By all counts, they told Sam Portaro, my father's kidneys should have given out by now. But they didn't. Everyone was amazed. I wasn't. I have always known that God helps you when you need him the most. This was one of those times. God's hand was in my father's recovery, and three children were extremely thankful for the help.

CHAPTER SIX

When I returned to Radford for my senior year, I had a mixture of feelings over it being my last year at college. I was glad on the one hand because I felt I was needed back at home. But I loved being at Radford, away from all the worries and pressures of home. I had made some very special friendships, and I enjoyed them immensely. I felt like I never wanted college to end. I resumed my studies with a vengeance. I planned to do my student teaching in the spring quarter, and I was very excited about that.

My brother Richard was in his senior year of high school. He wanted to go into engineering and had decided to apply to Virginia Tech. He called me from home often, asking me questions about how to fill out forms for admission and financial aid. He also spoke about his concerns over our father. I could tell that Richard was very worried and felt that Daddy wasn't taking good care of himself. I decided to take a weekend trip home. It was mid-October, and not many students were planning trips home, especially when home was quite a distance away. My usual rides weren't available, so I searched the advertisement boards in the student union. I found one going to Yorktown. That was only a twenty-minute ride down the Colonial Parkway from my house. Daddy and my brothers could meet me, they said. I took the ride. I had very mixed feelings about accepting a five-hour ride home with strangers. But I had this sense of urgency about being home. Somewhere deep inside me, I felt this voice telling me to get home.

I survived the trip. I had to listen to weird music and long conversations about who was dating whom, none of which I knew, but I made it. We arrived in Yorktown around four in the afternoon. Daddy and the boys were waiting for me under the big bridge as we had discussed. It was so good to see them, and they were very happy to see me. I noticed that Daddy looked thinner and seemed very tired. There were great, dark bags under his eyes. We drove home, and I cooked a simple meal, but Dad and the boys went on about it like I was some famous chef. The next day, I cleaned the house a bit and caught up with the laundry. Daddy dozed on and off all morning. He didn't eat much breakfast and only a small lunch. Donald was spending some time with my dad back in the master bedroom. Richard wandered back there to ask a question. I was in the kitchen cleaning up from lunch. Suddenly I heard a guttural scream from Richard. "Liz, oh my god! Liz!" Pins and needles exploded inside my head. I virtually flew to the back of the house. Those little fireworks were going off inside my head again. My heart was pounding so hard, almost up into my throat. I rushed into my dad's bedroom and saw him lying on the bed, shaking; his eyes were rolled into the back of his head. His color was pale white, with almost a bluish tinge. I realized immediately that he was having convulsions. I probably said "Oh my god" too because that is what I always say when I find myself in a horrible emergency situation. I say it without even thinking. It is like a ritualistic call for help.

"Daddy is dying. He's dying!" Donald screamed.

"Not if we can help it!" I grabbed Daddy's shoulder and tried to revive him. Richard listened to his chest.

"I think he has stopped breathing," he cried. "And I can't hear his heartbeat. We have to do CPR!"

Richard, an Eagle Scout, began to take the proper steps to resuscitate our father. "Donald, you run. Go call the ambulance, and hurry!" I shouted. Richard blew breaths into our father as I pumped his chest. I don't remember how long we worked at this, five minutes or less perhaps. Just as the paramedics arrived, we started to see our dad begin to come around. Richard explained to them exactly what had happened. His words came rushing quickly as he related the details. He had been talking to Daddy when he seemed to drift off suddenly. Then Daddy reared back on the bed, turning around to talk to the corner of the ceiling near the head of the bed. "I'm coming, honey. I'm coming to be with you." Richard and Donald watched with open, huge eyes, mouths agape, convinced our father was having a vision of our mother. Then after saying those words, Daddy had fallen back onto the bed and gone into convulsions. That was when Richard had screamed for me to come help, and I had told Donald to call 911.

After telling them all we knew about what had happened and answering their questions about his medications and who was his local doctor, we left the room and allowed them to work on our dad. I remember Daddy looking up at me with his sad eyes as I turned to leave the room. We went down the hall into the living room. I sat, almost melting into the chair. I became suddenly aware of my tight muscles and drained energy. Richard was very upset. He kept talking about how Daddy had seen a vision of Momma and wanted to go be with her. That was Richard's greatest fear, losing Daddy. I tried to console him. "You were great, Rich," I said. "I couldn't have brought him back without you." I turned to Donald. "You were great too. You made that phone call, and they got here so fast!" I tried to manage a reassuring smile. Then a paramedic came into the room. "Do you have some orange juice?" he asked. I said that we did and got it for him. "We have your dad's doctor on the phone for some background information," he told me.

"You may want to talk to him." Feeling some relief at that news, I went over and picked up the extension as directed. I recognized Dr. Brown's voice right away. The paramedic was telling him my dad's symptoms, and I did not want to interrupt. I listened quietly, waiting for just the right moment to let my presence be known, but that moment never came. As I listened, I couldn't believe what I heard. My face became flushed as my anger flared. "It sounds like," Dr. Brown was saying, "Mr. Tisdale suffered from too much insulin in his system, and the kids got hysterical. Clearly they overreacted." He went on to tell what dosage to give, but I wasn't listening carefully anymore. His words kept repeating themselves over and over in my mind. *Overreacted. Overreacted?* I was livid! I quietly replaced the telephone receiver. Dr. Brown had been my father's doctor for years. I had never cared for his abrupt bedside manner, but my father trusted him completely. He knew all that we had been through as a family and all the suffering my father had been through over the years. How dare he belittle what we had just gone through! He hadn't been here. He hadn't seen our father convulse and seem to stop breathing. I was so angry. I couldn't wait for the paramedics to leave our house. When they came out from the room, they had Daddy on a gurney. They told me they were taking him to the hospital for observation. I was so surprised. I hadn't counted on this development at all. If this had been a case of kids overreacting, why did Daddy have to go to the hospital? I wondered. What would I do about having to go back to school on Sunday? How could I just leave? What about my brothers?

I made some phone calls to the family. My great-aunt Geneva, who lived in Richmond, offered to come and stay with my brothers for a few days. That was a great relief. We found out later that Daddy would be released from the hospital on Monday afternoon. He had not been eating properly but had still taken his regular dose of insulin. There had not been enough sugar in his system, and that had caused the seizure. The bottom line was that he needed to take better care of himself.

On Sunday afternoon, Richard drove me the twenty-minute drive to meet my ride. I was very uneasy leaving them, but I felt I had no other choice. But my great-aunt Geneva made sure that my brothers and my dad would be all right before she left them. She stayed the rest of the week and went home the following weekend. Daddy did better with taking care of himself. We had another memorable Christmas, and I returned to school after the holiday break, ready to concentrate on student teaching and graduation. I had put off taking an algebra class, the last of my required math courses, and it was hanging over my head.

CHAPTER SEVEN

The new year of 1983 arrived with a new sense of hope. It was the year I was to graduate from college. I planned to seek a teaching job in Williamsburg after graduation and go home to live with Daddy and Donald, as Richard would be preparing to attend Virginia Tech as a freshman. He had already been accepted, and I thought it would be an easy transition as we swapped roles of being the oldest at home to care for everything. I hadn't dated much during my years at Radford so far, and I felt downhearted about the possibility of meeting someone special before graduation in the spring. An important turn of events came one mid-January evening that year. My very best college friend, Adaline, had talked me into going on a shopping trip to Roanoke one Saturday afternoon. She had made arrangements with another friend of hers named Phil to meet us for dinner around seven that evening. Phil's home was in Roanoke, and he had gone home to visit for the weekend with one of his suitemates. Neither Adaline nor I had ever met Phil's friend. Adaline loved meeting new people and was delighted with the idea of meeting for dinner. I was a bit less enthusiastic about the whole arrangement. My fondness for Phil was much smaller than Adaline's. He could be loud and overbearing, and worst of all, he was possessive of his friendship with Adaline. I figured that this young man he would bring along could be no better. Deep down, I sensed my feelings about Phil were a bit unreasonable. He really was fun to be around most of the time. He had a hearty, jolly laugh and was always full of ideas for fun things to do. He could be described as a ball of energy, really, and he just wore one out after a while. What I wasn't willing to admit to myself was that I was a bit resentful of his friendship with Adaline. It meant less time that she could spend with me, and we had always done practically everything together since we met in our first year at Radford. She was my dearest, closest friend. She knew everything I had been through. We told each other everything. There was so much I admired about her. She had such charisma and could befriend anybody, but she had chosen me to be her best friend. I was also a little wary of Phil's motives toward Adaline. He didn't seem to want a romantic relationship with her, and yet he wanted to go everywhere and do everything with her. Sometimes I felt like he was more of a leech than a friend to her. I knew I wasn't the only one in our circle of close friends who worried about Phil's intentions toward Adaline.

Nevertheless, I pushed aside my unenthusiastic feelings, and we met at a restaurant outside the mall. It was called Mac and Maggie's, and it was a fun sort of place attended by many of the college crowd. Adaline and I arrived first and were seated in a booth. Minutes later, when Phil and his friend arrived, I eyed the one I didn't know too well. He seemed younger. I wondered how much. But there was something different about him too, something about his eyes. I studied him through lowered lashes. Was that a gleam of honesty mixed with determination that I detected? The look in his eyes and the set of his jaw was in direct contrast to the rest of his body language, which showed rigid attempts to cover up his uneasiness. I soon learned that he was a freshman. That accounted for his feelings of insecurity around us seniors! And he was from Northern Virginia. Well, that counted against him in my mind, because after dealing with Leslie, my third roommate from my freshman year, I didn't have the best impression of people from Northern Virginia. He dressed very well, I noticed. He was wearing a pair of golfing-type athletic shoes I had never seen before. They said PONY on them. I hadn't heard of them before. He fit into what Adaline and I would call the tall-dark-and-handsome category. Adaline pinched me under the table. I knew what that meant. She thought he was cute. We ordered drinks and talked a bit. Adaline smiled and tossed her hair, laughing in a full-throated way at most of what our male companions said.

She always did that. She could get along with anyone. No one was a stranger to Adaline. I often wished I could be more like her in that way. But I was less gregarious, preferring to appear aloof and sophisticated, or so I thought. We learned that his name was George Armstrong. I had never met a George this young before. I was a bit intrigued by him without really understanding why. He was from a family of seven children, and he was a twin. I was impressed about him being a twin despite myself. I had a special interest in twins because of my mother.

After a while, Adaline and I excused ourselves to go to the ladies' room. "Oh my god!" Adaline shrieked once we were inside the restroom, out of hearing range. "He is so adorable," she went on.

I continued to act aloof and uninterested. "Oh, Adaline, he's a baby! He is just a freshman," I said. She laughed. "I don't care! I want to get to know him better. I think he might like me," she went on. "Well, he doesn't seem to like me," I stated. And I knew I had not really given him any cause to be interested in me. I acted cool and distant, though not in a mean way. When we returned to the table, I laughed and enjoyed myself with them, but I did not bubble all over the boys the way Adaline did. She had that kind of personality. She got along with everyone, and everyone loved her.

Adaline and Phil decided after dinner that we should find another establishment that had a livelier crowd, where we might go dancing. Phil chose a place farther down town in Roanoke. As we got into the car to follow Phil and George to the club, I voiced my concerns. "I don't know about this Adaline," I said doubtfully. "You'll hang out with Phil, and I'll be left alone with George. He probably thinks I'm stuck-up." She laughed it off. "Oh no, he doesn't. Just talk to him. Let your guard down!" she advised me. So as the night wore on, I did relax more as I talked with George. I realized that he was really nothing like Phil, as I had feared, and I found that I actually enjoyed his company a lot. He was different than most young men his age. He was easy to talk to, and I felt comfortable around him. I didn't feel like I had to pretend to be something I wasn't. That was so refreshing to me especially since I had so many heavy things on my shoulders that most people my age never even dreamed of dealing with.

As the winter turned into spring, my friendship with George blossomed just like a pink-petaled cherry tree. He became a permanent fixture in our dormitory after classes, along with Phil, who couldn't leave Adaline alone for one minute, it seemed to me. I was busy with my student teaching. I loved every minute of it and knew in my heart I was meant to be a teacher. I worked with a wonderful kindergarten teacher whose wisdom I still draw from today. When my responsibilities at the elementary school were over, I would hurry back to campus to have dinner with the gang. as we lovingly referred to ourselves. I didn't really admit it to myself at the time, but I mostly looked forward to seeing George every evening. With all that I was involved in at college, it was easy to put my family worries aside. I spoke with my dad every Sunday, and he always assured me that things were fine. I didn't question it. I wanted everything to be fine and normal. This seemed like the most fabulous time of my life; and I, like Cinderella, didn't want the clock to strike midnight.

In reality, my dad wasn't doing as well as he led me to believe. In early April, he began experiencing a lot of kidney problems. His kidneys were shutting down on him. It was because of the diabetes, and I'm sure stress played a role as well. He had to be hospitalized, and he never let me know. He called his aunt Geneva to come stay with my brothers. The hospital determined that my father needed extended care. He would have to have kidney dialysis twice a week to survive. A facility that could give that kind of extended care was not available in Williamsburg. The closest one available was in Norfolk. We knew from the previous summer that the best kidney doctors in Virginia were practicing in Norfolk, so at least he would be closer to them. All of the arrangements were made without my knowledge or opinion. I was furious when I finally found out. I felt as though my father had been locked away in some institution, torn from his children without their having a voice in the matter. I took out a lot of my frustration on the nurses and doctors I talked to long-distance, trying to get information about my dad's progress. It was hard to deal with the situation from so far away.

School was not over for another few weeks. Earlier, I had ended up dropping my evening algebra class because I was failing it. That meant I was one class shy of graduating on time. As difficult and frustrating as that reality was, I refused to let it get me down. I needed more time to focus and study on algebra. Too late, I realized I should have never put it off as I did. True to character, I was trying to take on too much. I planned that I could return in the fall, take the class, and then be done with it. I figured that it would be much easier if it was the only class I had to focus on. I hoped that this summer would be much like the last few had been. With my support and care, Daddy would be better and home by the end of August, when I would have to leave to take the class. Unlike the other years, I would come home at Christmas for good, having completed the class for graduation. Daddy wouldn't have to make it alone for an entire school year, just one semester. It seemed like a good plan to me. I counted on it coming true.

During this time, George was very supportive. I think he was in awe of all the responsibility I had on me. I never wanted that school year to end. My friends, except for George, were all graduating and moving on. My utopia at school was ending. I felt like a tightrope walker who has just lost her safety net. I cried a lot that sunny day of graduation. I had to watch George drive away with his dad to go home for the summer, and I worried whether I would ever see him again. I watched my three best friends in the whole world graduate without me. I felt so left out and so alone, standing next to them for picture taking, they wearing black caps and gowns and me in a white floral dress. Leaving Radford University that day was like leaving sanctuary. A family friend had come to bring me home from college. It was a very long drive home. I wondered what lay ahead for my brothers and me and my dad. I felt somehow that it wasn't going to be an easy summer for any of us. But I pushed my doubts away. I had a plan to make it all right. It was a good plan, I reasoned with myself.

Once home, I was again comforted by the sound of the cooing dove in the early mornings. As I had done each summer before, I tried to put the household back into some kind of routine again for my brothers while working full-time as an interpreter in Colonial Williamsburg. Since my father had been hospitalized, my great-aunt Geneva had been staying with my brothers, caring for them while

I was at Radford. I knew they felt shuffled around, and they were extremely glad I was home again. Richard was less than a month away from graduating from high school. He had done little more than filling out the paperwork in preparing to go away to college in the fall. I began putting things aside for him that I knew he would need. I reflected on the fun shopping trips Momma and I had taken together the summer before I had gone away to college. My heart ached for him in knowing that he would never get the chance to have that same special time with her. I knew I had to fill that void for both my brothers. I had promised her, and I had promised myself too. I slipped into her role easily. I instinctively knew what she would have done and how she would have wanted things to go in certain situations. She had been such a good teacher those eighteen years of my life. I wished that I was able to thank her for all she had taught me and to apologize for all the troubles I had caused her while growing up. Even though I felt she already knew as I raised my eyes toward heaven, I thought it would feel so much better if I could tell her in person. But the cooing of the dove sustained me. It was like a message from her every morning when I awoke, letting me know I would make it through the day, and that she would be watching over me.

CHAPTER EIGHT

Along with getting Richard ready to graduate, I was determined that Daddy would be able to attend the graduation. After talking with the doctors, I prepared to take on the task of overseeing a program of home dialysis for my father. He would receive a hospice-type service, where a trained professional was to come to our home to help with the dialysis twice a week. I will never forget the day the boxes of solutions were delivered. There were so many of them; they filled up our entire family room. The deliveryman kept carting in more and more until there was only room left for a small pathway in which to enter the room. After he left, I stood there among the stacks of boxes, which were taller than me. I suddenly felt a twinge of doubt and fear about whether I would be able to handle taking care of my father. But that feeling didn't last very long. I didn't allow it to. I pushed all doubts aside and continued planning for the summer. I was like the Little Engine That Could from the childhood story I loved. I knew if I kept thinking I could do all of this, I would be able to. I refused to give up and just plowed ahead. I needed to attend a short class to learn briefly how to use the dialysis equipment and also how to handle emergencies should they arise. I called the hospital and made arrangements to take the class.

All of the household responsibilities fell on me. I paid the bills. I bought the groceries. I cleaned the house. I urged my brothers to help. Donald was good with maintaining the yard. He enjoyed being outside and didn't mind cutting the grass. Richard was more difficult to persuade to help. He was excited about graduating and usually wanted to be off with his friends when he wasn't working at his summer job. Richard was finding it hard to deal with Daddy's declining health. He was petrified of losing Daddy. In a lot of ways, I felt similar to a single parent. When something went wrong, my brothers turned to me. I was so busy being a rock for everyone else I didn't count on my needing someone to be strong for me.

One drizzly morning in late May, not too long after I had returned home from Radford, Richard missed his bus and needed me to drive him to school. As luck would have it, it was one of my days off from work, and driving him would be no problem. I slipped into shorts and a T-shirt, pulled my hair back into a ponytail, and shoved my feet into my tennis shoes without socks. I didn't waste time putting on any makeup or jewelry. I planned to drive him up to the building and drop him off, then come straight home again. I got Richard to school with no problems. I was anxious to get back home quickly because I was expecting a phone call from George about whether he would be able to visit me for the weekend. I took a shortcut. I had to cross a busy intersection. After stopping, I looked carefully both ways, as I always did. I prided myself on being a careful driver. I remember seeing a large Budweiser delivery truck coming up from a safe distance on my right.

On my left, a large white Cadillac was turning into a parking lot, but no other car was in view. I proceeded out slowly. Almost immediately, I heard a loud horn blowing, and curiosity about where it was coming from flashed across my mind. Suddenly, it was as though someone had flipped a switch, and time began moving in slow motion. The echo of the blowing horn resonated over and over in my ears. I turned my head left, toward the direction of the sound. It was as though I was wrapped in fuzzy cotton batting. All light and sounds were muted. I felt a sudden violent impact, which threw me both forward and sideways. I hit my head on the steering wheel, but I didn't recall it at the time. I would come to realize it a day later when a large greenish bruise appeared on my forehead. The seatbelt buckle dug deeply into my right thigh as I was flung sideways over onto it. My mind was reeling as I tried to take in what had just happened. My car lumbered like a sick animal over to the opposite side of the road.

People swarmed all around, seeming to come up out of nowhere. I looked over at the car that had just hit me. It was a small pale yellow car, an older Toyota. Where had it come from? I had never seen it. Almost as an answer to my unspoken question, a man came running over to me as I got out of my car. He immediately asked me if I was okay. Numbly, I nodded. "There was no way you could have seen her coming," he told me. "I saw the whole thing! She sped out from behind that turning Cadillac," he continued. It was somehow comforting to know I had not been so careless in my driving, but as I looked at the damage to our family car, I had a huge panic attack. It was our only link to seeing Daddy! What in the world was I going to do? Daddy was in the hospital; I couldn't possibly tell him that I had wrecked the car. How would it affect him? And whom could I turn to now for help? I felt such despair. My hands were shaking, and they felt so cold. Goose bumps pimpled my arms and legs. I felt random raindrops fall as the drizzle turned to rain. The right front tire of our car was pushed over to one side, and I could see that the axle was severely bent. The car was not drivable, I was sure.

A business office, located on the corner where the accident had happened, allowed us to go inside, out of the rain. I sat in a chair, waiting for an officer to come talk to me. Other people were sitting around the office, murmuring about what had happened. I felt sick to my stomach. I couldn't stop shaking. I was so angry with myself for this mistake. *What am I going to do? What am I going to do?* I couldn't stop the panicked thoughts in my head. I rocked back and forth in the chair, hugging myself and running my hands up and down my arms to try to warm up. Finally, an officer came in to talk with me. She had taken statements from three witnesses. She asked me to step outside with her and tell her what had happened.

By now the rain had almost stopped. There was just a fine mist in the air. I told her everything I remembered. She was very kind, and even understanding about my not seeing the other car. Her soft-spoken voice helped to calm me down a bit. It was such a relief that she was not treating me like some careless, reckless kid. I looked down at my clothes. I certainly wasn't dressed like a respectable adult. I was hoping the man's statement about my not being able to see the car coming would help. But as it turned out, I was still charged with failure to yield the right of way. I don't know if the other driver was even charged with speeding, though it seemed obvious to me and to the other witnesses that she had been. Her luck had not been as good as mine, so it seemed. She had been hurt in the accident. She suffered a broken wrist and had a minor whiplash. She also knocked out a tooth when she hit the steering wheel. I felt bad about her getting hurt, but at the same time, I felt strongly that she contributed to the accident by being in too much of a hurry to get to work. The officer told me that the woman had admitted to running a bit late that morning. I watched as the paramedics took the injured woman out of the car and loaded her onto a gurney. Instinctively, I walked up to her and said, "I'm so sorry. I hope you will be okay." I could tell by the tight lines on her face that she was in pain. She said, "Thank you." Then they put her into the back of the ambulance and closed the doors.

The accident had happened only about one mile or so from my house. The rain had picked up again, and I asked the officer if she could take me home. She told me that it was against policy and suggested I should call someone to come get me. I nodded my understanding and turned away so she couldn't see the tears pool in my eyes. There was no one to call.

I walked home alone in the rain. Both raindrops and tears rolled down my cheeks as I walked the single mile home. I felt so alone in a great big world. It was so hard to be an adult. It was so hard to be the one in charge and have the family's well-being rest on your shoulders when you're only twenty-one. Daddy had always been the one to make it all better. I could always count on him when the going got tough. But our roles had reversed, and he was counting on me to take care of things. I had promised Momma that I would. I felt like I had let everyone down. This day was a great low for me. I got to the house and went to my room to change clothes. I was soaking wet. I dried my hair and set my mind to thinking about how I would overcome this new hurdle. I knew it would not be good to tell Daddy, at least not right away. I would wait until the car was fixed and tell him as an afterthought. George was the first person I wanted to have help me. I called him and told him the whole story. He said he was planning on coming for the weekend anyway; he would just leave a few hours earlier. He told me he would be at my house in two hours. Waves of relief and hopefulness washed over me. I began to feel better right away.

Next, I called my good friend Lou Ann, who lived around the corner from me. We had grown up together and had a very close friendship. I wasn't sure she would be home, but she was, and she came right over. She helped me straighten up the house a bit and waited with me until George arrived. I was starting to feel the effects of having been in a car accident. My whole body ached. When George arrived, he was like a savior. He knew exactly what to do. He called the body shop to find out the estimate. He helped me call the insurance company about the accident, and then he suggested calling the dealer who had sold me the car last summer. George thought that since the salesman had been so understanding about our situation, perhaps he would help us out with a loaner car. His instincts turned out to be right on target. Later that day, a used sedan was sent to our house for us to drive while our car was in the body shop for about two weeks. By the end of the day, all the loose ends were tied up, and I felt a great sense of relief. And I felt like I owed all that relief to George.

CHAPTER NINE

My father had been moved to an extended-care facility in Norfolk just two weeks before I came home from college. It was called Lake Taylor Hospital, and it was an older building not too far from a newer hospital where the best kidney doctors in Virginia practiced. While it was a good situation for my dad, it was difficult for my brothers and me. My work schedule didn't allow for us to drive to see Daddy every day. Twice during the week was about all we could manage, and then weekends too. We called him on the phone every day, though, and usually he was physically able to talk to us. The trip to see Dad was at least an hour one way on a good day. The traffic on the interstate was heavy, especially in the summer with vacationers heading toward the beaches of Virginia and North Carolina. Going through the Hampton Roads Tunnel was the trickiest part of the trip. Timing was everything in trying to avoid the heaviest traffic. Sometimes it didn't matter how you tried to time the trip; the tunnel would be backed up anyway from some accident or roadwork. Those trips with Richard and Donald were fun, though. We opened all the windows and turned up the radio, singing to the popular tunes as the wind blew through our hair. We talked about things we wanted to do and confided our feelings to each other. We bonded a lot on those trips.

We greatly enjoyed spending time with our dad, but not at Lake Taylor. That hospital seemed to house the most pitiful of cases, mostly older people, but some young children too with horrible afflictions. The hallways were drab, medical green and cream color, and there never seemed to be enough sunlight coming into the place. You didn't see a lot of smiles there from either the nursing staff or the patients. It seemed to be a place where people went to wait on dying, and I did not like to think of my father in those circumstances. Often Daddy seemed weak and fragile, but he lit up like a Christmas tree when we would arrive to visit with him. We would often take him for wheelchair rides onto the grounds for fresh air when the weather wasn't too hot. Daddy didn't like the hospital food there too much and often would ask us to bring him a fish sandwich from Burger King with just mustard and onions on it. He craved those, and I doubted if the nursing staff would have approved it had they known we snuck those sandwiches to our dad. But his eyes sparkled so much while he ate them. Sometimes a little bit of mustard would dribble down out of the corner of his mouth. I focused on his enjoyment of the food rather than on how he seemed to be deteriorating. Daddy loved watermelon too, and often I brought a Tupperware container to him filled with cubes of the fruit inside. The nurses approved of that treat and showed rare smiles when they saw my dad eating the fruit. I wanted so badly for my dad to come home and have the in-home dialysis treatments like I had planned, but clearly, he was too weak for that just yet. He was so thin too, and sometimes lethargic. He was only allowed to go home for weekends on what they called furloughs, and his doctor rarely issued him a weekend pass. But Richard's graduation was fast approaching, and Daddy had to be able to attend.

With the help of my Uncle Don, we were able to obtain a weekend pass for my dad to attend Richard's graduation in mid-June. Daddy was still weak and unable to use his prosthesis. He had lost too much weight, and it no longer fit properly. He wasn't strong enough to use crutches either, so he remained in a wheelchair. I knew it meant so much to Richard for Dad to be there. Daddy was very proud of Richard, and it would have been a crushing blow to both of them if Dad couldn't have come home for such an important occasion. Of course, Uncle Don and Aunt Kay were there, and my cousins. I felt strange being back in my high school again. I felt so different about myself. I had changed a lot in four years. As I sat watching the ceremony, so many emotions washed over me. I felt like my mother's presence was there with us too. As I sat there in the auditorium between my father and Donald, listening to the *Pomp and Circumstance* play, tears welled up. I felt like I was a viewing glass for my mother. As though somehow I helped her to see what was going on, and I felt the emotions that she would be feeling as she watched her son cross the stage to graduate. The sense of pride I felt was too overwhelming to be mine alone. I was so happy that my dad managed to overcome great odds and be able to attend with us. I was so thankful that Richard would have this moment in time to remember and cherish. The emotions were so strong; I felt as though I might burst.

After Richard's graduation, it seemed as though Daddy's condition improved somewhat. He seemed a bit stronger when we would visit, and he sounded better on the phone, often joking and laughing. I got up the nerve to tell him about the car accident I'd had, and he took it well. I also told him a bit about George, and he said he would like to meet him sometime. I felt Dad's condition was going well enough that I could get away for one quick weekend visit to see George. He had invited me earlier, but I had not yet had an opportunity to accept until after Richard's graduation. It would be the first time I had met his mother and the rest of his family, as I'd already met his dad and his twin brother at Radford. I rode on a Greyhound bus for three hours up to Springfield, Virginia, where George met me at the station in the early afternoon. We were so excited to see each other that we neglected to get my luggage off the bus before it pulled away again. I panicked. But George took care of it. He talked to the man at the counter inside the station, and we were told that the suitcase would be dropped off there later on in the evening after seven o'clock. We would have to return for it.

With that solved, we hopped into George's little red Vega and drove off. It was a wonderful adventure for me to be in the busy Northern Virginia area. George was wonderful at showing me the sights and telling me stories of things he had done growing up there. After a short sightseeing tour, we pulled into the driveway of his home, and I was immediately struck by the fact that we seemed to come from the same kinds of backgrounds. His neighborhood was similar to the one I had grown up in, only much larger. The white, ranch-style house sat on a very green and neatly manicured lawn. There were several cars in the driveway. George said that with seven children, the drive often looked like a parking lot. My heart pounded in my chest as I prepared to meet his mother. It was so important to me that she like me. George took me inside the house through a side door, and I stepped into a large kitchen area. I noticed how neat and clean and orderly it was, and then there she was. George, I realized, looked very much like his mother. Martha Armstrong smiled and gave me a big hug. It was a strong, sturdy kind of hug with no hint of hesitation. She made me feel very welcome. She had us sit down at the big kitchen table and offered me a drink. She wanted to know how my trip had been. George began to tell her the silly story of how we temporarily lost my luggage.

The weekend was wonderful and went by all too quickly. George took me sightseeing downtown, and we shopped at the big mall near his home. I had never seen a mall so large before. He had a few of his close high school friends over to meet me, and they talked about all the crazy things they had done together throughout high school. I realized how sheltered my life in Williamsburg had been in comparison, but I kept that to myself. I really enjoyed getting to know George better. We made plans for George to come visit me next for the Fourth of July weekend. My birthday was coming up, and he wanted to celebrate with me. And he also wanted to meet my dad.

Once home again, I arranged another weekend pass for Daddy since I had been away visiting George. Dad was excited to come home again with us. He talked a lot about how much he missed being home. As luck would have it, the tunnel was blocked by an accident, and we sat in traffic for over two hours before finally getting home. I was terribly angry and frustrated, but Daddy took it all in stride. He said he was just glad to be with us. We spent as much time as possible with him over the weekend. Donald and Dad worked up in the attic on his train set some of the time. But I noticed that as the weekend wore on, Daddy became more tired and drained. I could tell that his body needed dialysis. That was very troubling to me since I wanted him to get well enough to be able to stay at home and not have to return to Lake Taylor. I refused to let it get me down. I remained optimistic. I didn't want to examine the alternatives too closely.

The week before my birthday went by quickly. I was going to be twenty-two this year. As planned, George was coming to visit and help me celebrate. I was so excited about seeing him again, and I was anxious for Daddy to meet George. My dad's condition had taken a downhill turn since his recent weekend pass. He had periods of forgetfulness and seemed more weak and tired than before. His doctor had asked me to make time to come talk with him. I arranged to do so after my birthday. I didn't want to put a damper on my special weekend. I had made every effort to get the house clean and neat for George's arrival. The only room I couldn't do anything with was the den. It was still stacked high with the boxes of solution for home dialysis. Having them in there seemed to be a sign that we hadn't given up hope.

Being with George again took away some of the tension and stress I endured. I was able to laugh and feel carefree. I didn't think about *why* so much, but it was very important to me that George meet my dad. On my birthday, Richard, Donald, George, and I all drove together to Lake Taylor. I had told George all about the hospital, but I don't think he was really prepared for how it made him feel. Unlike my brothers and me, George had not dealt with a lot of family illnesses. I could tell that the hospital made him feel uncomfortable. Not that dealing with illnesses makes you more comfortable really, maybe just a bit more tolerant and prepared. We walked down the bleak hallways toward the back of the hospital where Dad's room was. Daddy seemed a bit more alert than he had been at our last visit, but he was still not quite himself. He sat up in the bed when we walked into the room. "Hello, hello there," he greeted us with a smile. His speech was slow and deliberate, as though he had recently woken up from a nap. Richard and Donald were eager to give him hugs and take advantage of his bright mood. I could feel my pulse beating rapidly and wasn't able to manage containing the broad smile on my face.

"I've got someone with me I want you to meet," I told him. Daddy's eyes were as blue as I had ever seen them, a beautiful Mediterranean blue. He stared up at me for a moment as though he was trying to take it all in. I pulled George by the arm over closer to the bed. Daddy turned his head away from me and fixed his eyes on George. He stared at George with half a smile as though he knew some secret we weren't in on. His eyes were transfixed on George's face, and I watched Daddy with the same intensity. There was such a moment of clarity in his eyes, a spark of wisdom not usually there of late, and his eyes seemed even bluer. "You'll take good care of my baby girl, won't you?" he asked, only it was more of a statement than a question. I suddenly felt like my father knew something about my future that I wasn't privy to. George answered, yes, he would do his best to take good care of me. Daddy smiled and nodded, closing his eyes. He patted George's hand. Then just as suddenly, the extraordinary moment was gone. The conversation went in another direction as a nurse came in to check on Dad and encourage us to take him outside for some fresh air. While I got Daddy ready to go outside, George went with my brothers to the nearby Burger King to get the familiar treat of a fish sandwich with mustard and onions. The nurse had to help get Daddy into the wheelchair. It was slow going since he was so weak from the constant dialysis treatments.

Finally, he was ready. I wheeled him down the hallway to a door that lead out to a garden path. We settled under a tree, where there was a large bench for me to sit on. It was cooler in the shade. A small breeze rustled the leaves of the tree now and then. It was nice to have my dad all to myself for a few moments. I pulled out a little package from my purse. "You want to see what you got me for my birthday?" I joked. Daddy knew I had seen a jade necklace in a catalogue because I had mentioned it several times before. He had encouraged me to go ahead and buy it for myself. It was no surprise when I pulled it out of the white box. "So that's it?" he asked. "It is pretty. It reminds me of your Momma. I hope it wasn't too much."

"Not at all," I said truthfully. "It was a bargain, just thirty dollars. And I love it." I put it on. "See, doesn't it look great?" Dad agreed that it did. Then he asked, "You really like this George, don't you?"

I smiled. "Yes. He has been a great friend to me. I've never met anyone quite like him before."

"That's good," was his response. Then the boys and George returned from their errand. Daddy gratefully enjoyed his favorite sandwich. George got a kick out of watching how much pleasure that sandwich brought my father. Soon, however, we could see that

Daddy was beginning to tire. After he finished eating, we took him back to his room and settled him back into his bed again. It was especially hard for Richard and Donald to have to leave him each time we visited. They lingered, hugging him and trying to talk to him a bit more. He began to drift off to sleep even before we left the room. We told him good-bye and promised to visit again in a couple of days. The entire trip back to Williamsburg was filled with conversations of the hospital and how we wished to get Dad out of there as soon as possible.

CHAPTER TEN

Several days after that birthday visit, I had my scheduled appointment with my father's doctor. Dr. Weinstein always wore a flashy gold chain around his neck and a heavy gold watch on his wrist, but he was a nice man and seemed to really care about my dad. Dr. Weinstein explained to me that my father's kidneys were deteriorating more and more all the time. He told me that my dad had made it to a point that he could not live without dialysis, and he was needing it more frequently than before. Dr. Weinstein did not think my dad would recover from this present kidney shutdown as he had last summer. He, like other doctors before him, said that he thought it was a miracle that my father had lived as long as he had. My natural response was to say that Daddy would most likely recover this time too. He had defied the odds before and could do it again. But the doctor shook his head. "No," he said, "I don't think so. Elizabeth, your family has a tough choice ahead of you. I cannot continue treating your father as I am without being totally honest with you. I truly feel that the dialysis procedure we perform every other day on your father is now simply putting off death rather than sustaining life. Your father is enduring pain that he doesn't have to, and his quality of life is not what I think you would want for him."

Those little fireworks were going off inside my head again. I really didn't want to hear the words that Dr. Weinstein was saying, but I didn't want my father to suffer either. I maintained my composure with more ease than I thought possible. I had a lot of questions. "But he is alert and having some really good days," I said. "You really don't think he could recover enough to come home and I could do that home dialysis I made arrangements for?" Again, Dr. Weinstein shook his head. "Of course, anything can happen. Your father has proven that to me time and time again. But my best medical opinion is no. You see, your father's kidneys are very deteriorated. They will never heal enough for him to return to a normal life. Usually, that would mean he would need a kidney transplant operation, but I know he probably wouldn't survive such a surgery, given his fragile condition. Those kinds of surgeries are for prolonging a healthy life. As it is, we are just prolonging his pain right now, and I see no medical way of making him any better. If I had to make this decision about my father, I would take him off the dialysis treatment altogether and let nature take its course. If a miracle happens, that would be wonderful, but in all likelihood, your father will pass away within several days after being removed from the machines and finally have peace. I just can't see prolonging his pain any further."

I sat a moment quietly, thinking, trying to take it all in. It felt like this doctor had just set a massive boulder down on my shoulders. "This is not a decision I can make by myself," I told him. "My brothers and I must agree about this, and as long as my dad is alert and seemingly happy, I feel sure my brothers will be strongly against this idea."

"I understand," he answered. "If they want, I can explain all this to them in person. I'd be happy to talk to any member of your family about this. I know it won't be any easy decision, and I don't think it is a decision that you and your brothers should make alone. Talk to your whole family about this."

"Thank you," I said. "I will talk to them, and then we will give my dad a few weeks to see how he does. More than anything, I want to do what is right for my father. His progress in the coming weeks will have to guide me."

Dr. Weinstein agreed and told me that if at any time we decided to take my dad off the machine, we were just to call his office and give our permission. "Don't I need to sign a bunch of papers?" I asked.

"No," he said. "There is no need to put you through all that. We will just discontinue the dialysis treatments, in the best interest of your father, and your family too. Then we will wait and see what happens."

I certainly had a lot to think about on the hour-long ride home. I knew I would have a very hard time explaining this new development to Richard and Donald. They had such a hard time putting aside emotion when it came to our dad. What child wouldn't, though? And they were just children—Richard about a month away from turning eighteen and Donald only fifteen. This was like a nightmare! Like something from a TV show. This issue was often the subject of a medical drama on television: family members having to decide whether to pull the plug on a loved one who would never be themselves again. I couldn't believe I was facing a very similar decision myself. I couldn't bear the thought of making Daddy suffer simply for my own self-centered needs. I knew how deeply he missed my mother. His life would never be the same without her, and he seemed to keep holding on for the sake of the three of us kids. But going through with this would make everything so final. We would really be alone. No more parents at all. *Orphans.* That was a terrifying thought. But I kept thinking of how much Daddy missed Momma and how he would be able to be with her again, and what joy and peace that would bring to him. Maybe the time had come. I sent up a few prayers as I pulled into our driveway and prepared myself for a talk with my brothers.

It was as difficult a conversation, as I had anticipated. Richard was especially hostile toward the thought of taking Daddy off dialysis. Anger oozed out of his every pore as he loudly denounced any part of the plan. Donald also didn't like the idea, but was less violent in his opposition. It was the first time we had ever thought about giving up on recovery for our father. Always, we had been his team of cheerleaders, always optimistic, always full of hope and faith in his pulling through each traumatic event of the past four years. None of us wanted to face what doing something like what Dr. Weinstein suggested meant. I knew I had to get beyond the anger and hurt my brothers were feeling and help them see clearly the choices we had before us. I took a deep breath.

"Look," I began again, "I would never suggest that Daddy is ready to give up his fight. We all agree that he is too full of life right now to even seriously consider this. But if those circumstances change, if he becomes less of the man we love so much, to the point he is only suffering if we keep him alive, well then, we owe it to him to think about this choice. We will just have to allow *him* to be our guide."

I waited to see what they would say. Would Richard return a quick, angry retort, or would he agree with me? Richard was really the key. Donald would usually follow my lead, within reason. Richard had been looking down at the floor while I had been talking. He raised his head, and I saw his eyes were full of tears. "Okay," he said quietly, "but I will only consider this if Daddy's condition changes *severely* for the worse. He doesn't deserve to suffer, but he also deserves every chance to recover, even a *microscopic* chance." Richard emphasized chosen words forcefully, and his eyes flashed with emotion.

"I think so too," I said and then looked toward Donald. He nodded his head in agreement.

Needless to say, thoughts of Dr. Weinstein's proposal haunted us at every visit to Lake Taylor.

At least it did for me. We didn't bring up the subject very much, except to say how we thought Daddy was doing. As July came to an end, Dad remained about the same, except he did seem to be a bit more forgetful and tired. I talked to my Uncle Don and Aunt Kay about what Dr. Weinstein had suggested. They seemed surprised, and troubled, by the thought of it. Aunt Kay especially was disturbed about three children having to decide the fate of their only living parent. I thought about it often and prayed for the strength to make the right decision.

It was around the first week of August that Daddy's condition took a downhill turn. We were on our usual weekend visit. I had taken him a container of fresh watermelon cubes, and I knew he would be so appreciative. He seemed drugged when we entered his room. He smiled and was so happy to see us, but he had a hard time sitting up and seemed extremely disoriented and groggy. He knew our names, though, and we were able to have a fairly good visit. I was troubled by the change in him. I asked the nurse about Dad's grogginess, and she said he had been that way for a couple days. I was frustrated further at hearing this. I wished the nurses would call me with any changes, but they never did. It wasn't that kind of hospital.

Our next visit was about three days later. Daddy slept through most of the time we were there. He aroused briefly a couple times, but he never carried on a conversation with us. We were all upset by this visit, and I wondered if this was the turn for the worse we had talked about. But I didn't broach the subject with my brothers. The next time we went to see Daddy, he was much more alert, and we talked and joked with him. That visit was filled with an unspoken sense of relief and renewed hope for the three of us. On the way home, Richard joked, "I knew Daddy had it in him. Those old doctors don't know him like we do. He's a fighter! Daddy will pull through this. I knew if I prayed hard enough, he could do it!" We all laughed. We felt so hopeful and lighthearted. All the windows were rolled down in the car, and we cranked the stereo, singing "Freeze Frame" at the top of our lungs.

It turned out that we really needed that special visit with our dad because the visits that followed that one were nowhere near as good. That was probably the last really alert visit we had with our father. He slept through the next three. The nurse on duty told me they suspected Daddy might be slipping into a coma. Those subsequent visits were agonizing for the three of us. We knew without voicing it what all this was leading to. By August 12 or so, we knew Daddy was not getting better. His color wasn't good, and he rarely woke up. If he did, he wasn't lucid enough to carry on a conversation with us. We took turns whispering to him our own special thoughts, hoping that he could hear us somehow. I had a difficult time seeing him in this condition. I had begun to hate visiting him. I just wanted it to be over. I didn't like the thought of him suffering. But I really didn't know what it would mean to us. I was so naive about what being orphaned would be like. I was more or less playacting at running a household and being the head of the family. It seemed so easy to me to step into my father's shoes and carry on. I faced it all with a bravery born out of ignorance, because I didn't really understand what I would be getting myself into.

Richard fought the weakening of our father with all his might. It tore him apart to see Daddy getting worse. At every visit, Richard would sit by the bed, holding Daddy's hand, whispering words of encouragement to him to hang in there and keep fighting. It was the most agonizing picture for me to watch. But at this latest visit, Richard hung his head in defeat and wept at the bedside. He whispered to Daddy that he could pass on peacefully and go be with Momma again. Donald stood on the other side of the bed, patting Daddy's hand in his own. I stood at the foot of the bed, caressing Daddy's foot under the covers. Daddy never opened his eyes or gave us any sign that he heard us or understood anything we said. As difficult as this moment was, another hard task still lay ahead of me.

CHAPTER ELEVEN

I called Dr. Weinstein's office the morning of August 15. I was told that the doctor was with a patient, and I could leave a message. I told the receptionist that the Tisdale family had decided to discontinue the dialysis treatment, as Dr. Weinstein had suggested, since Mr. Tisdale's condition continued to worsen. I told her to have the doctor call me if he had any questions about our decision. He never did.

My brothers and I never spoke of the decision after that day. We continued working and going about our business as usual. I could hardly bring myself to plan another visit, but I knew we needed to. I was very busy with work at the height of the tourist season, so I decided we would go in a few days, on a Saturday. I told George about our decision, and he made me promise to call him with any news, day or night. It was such a comfort to know he cared and supported me in all I was going through. We were both excited about the end of August approaching because it meant going back to Radford and being able to see each other every day again. I had so much on my mind, and I had trouble going to sleep each night. I wanted a crystal ball to tell me what the future held. I wanted the trauma of all we were going through to end, but I was afraid of it all coming to an end as well. I felt like I was on top of a giant snowball that was gathering speed as it went downhill. I busied myself with work and chores around the house. Keeping up a normal routine helped me feel a bit more sane. It was difficult not to drive myself crazy with the worrying and the wondering.

I finally went to sleep late, after tossing and turning one night, three days later. I slept fitfully at first, but finally found deep sleep sometime after midnight. It was from that deep dreamlike state that I was suddenly jolted awake by the ringing of the telephone. It was still pitch black outside, and I quickly flipped on the light beside my bed, squinting in the brightness of the sudden light. Almost five in the morning, I noticed as I glanced at the clock, and an immediate panicked feeling grabbed my chest. With a great sense of dread, I picked up the receiver, knowing that a call at this hour could only mean the worst. "Hello?" I asked softly. A nurse from Lake Taylor identified herself.

"I am calling to let you know that Mr. Tisdale expired at four thirty-two a.m." That was all she said. I blinked. My mind felt numb. *Expired* . . . My brain felt fuzzy and slow. "Um . . . ," I started to question her, but suddenly, it hit me; and I realized what she meant. "Uh . . . okay . . . thank you for letting me know . . ." Words were slow to come out of my mouth. My throat felt dry and uncomfortable. I hung up the phone and just sat on my bed. I didn't move for some time, but my mind was reeling. Earlier in the night, when I had difficulty in falling asleep, crickets had been loudly serenading me under my window. But now the night was very still. There were no noises except for the soft whirring of my window fan. Daddy was gone. His pain was over, and I knew he was experiencing great joy at being together again with my mother somewhere in another realm we call heaven. But down here on earth, I felt small and alone.

The weight of caring for my father was suddenly lifted, but my shoulders didn't feel lighter. Instead, a heavier burden had replaced the first one. It was the weight of being in charge. I wasn't Daddy's little girl anymore. I couldn't run to him when things went wrong. My brothers and I had given our father wings of flight, and he was gone now to a better place. He was with my mother, which I knew in my heart gave him great happiness. I felt sudden misgivings about what we had done. The thoughts flickered through my mind like the shuffling of playing cards. *Had stopping dialysis been the right choice? Was Daddy mad at us? Should I have gone to see him sooner? Why didn't I make myself go visit him these last three days? I should have been with him, holding his hand! What was the matter with me?* I had been so angry that I'd missed seeing Momma before she died, and yet I had not made the effort to be with my father. I felt terrible guilt sweep over me as I realized I had let him die alone in that dreary hospital. Guilt and a deep sadness engulfed me like the shadow of storm clouds sweeping over the land. I sat huddled on my bed, crying softly so as not to awaken my brothers. It was so early, and there was no need to get them up yet. It wouldn't change the fact that he was gone. Nothing would. I decided to wait until at least 6:00 a.m. before telling anyone. That was a more decent hour, I decided.

I have little memory of how I passed that hour before telling anyone what had happened. I sat in the dark for a while, thinking and thinking about it all. Reality had momentarily gone on vacation, and I felt stranded in a dark ocean somewhere between childhood and adulthood, between my past and my present. I would have to leave behind the comfortable and familiar and embrace the unknown. As the sun began to rise on a new day, I woke my brothers to tell them the news of our father. I don't remember the words I used or their reaction. I remember them saying that they hadn't heard the phone ring. Then I remember calling George. It was 6:30 a.m. He answered the phone immediately even though it was so early, and he told me that he knew it would be me. "I'm so sorry," he kept saying to me. "I'll drive down right away." He said he would stay as long as I needed him. He was already fulfilling what my father had asked of him.

I planned the details of the funeral with my brothers and my uncles. Having gone through this for my mother four years earlier, the planning was somewhat easier. Assuming the leadership role came to me quite naturally, and I took responsibility for certain tasks as though I had always done them. I greeted mourners and family friends at the funeral home. I comforted my brothers. Without really knowing it, I had been practicing for this time for four years. Each year of college life, I had taken on more and more responsibilities, so now I took on this role with ease. It may have seemed I was not afraid of all that lay ahead of me, but I was. I was just trying not to show it. I kept myself so busy with family and household details that I allowed little time for worrying.

For visitation evening at the funeral home, I decided against wearing black, just as I had for my mother. I chose a tropical print dress of olive green and cream. It was one of my favorites. I also wore the new beaded jade necklace. I knew I looked good in this outfit, and I knew it would help me feel confident and help me carry myself well. When we arrived at the funeral home, I entered the room with the casket much differently than I had at my mother's viewing. I was not shocked at the sight of Daddy. I felt a strange sense of calm. George held my hand and gave me a reassuring half smile. We walked over closer to the casket. My brothers and I had chosen a real wooden casket for Dad. Richard had felt strongly that it was the most appropriate one for Daddy. I looked down lovingly at my dad. He looked a bit waxy, but not as much as Momma had looked. You couldn't really tell they had put much makeup on him. He was wearing his charcoal tweed suit, the very one he had worn to Momma's funeral. He looked very natural and at peace. I wanted so very much to take his hand, but that overwhelming, nagging fear was still there. I couldn't seem to shake it off and bring myself to touch him. George put his arms around my shoulders and whispered into my ear, "I'll give you a few minutes alone." Then he walked over to my brothers. I took a deep breath and whispered to my dad. "Please understand, Daddy. We just didn't want you to suffer anymore. We thought you needed to be with Momma again. I hope we did the right thing. I hope you are happy. I hope you are not mad or disappointed with us." I wished he could have answered me.

Daddy's funeral service was much like my mother's had been. It too was held at Bruton Parish Church. The weather was hot and humid. The summer sky was hazy and not so clear blue as it had been that October day for my mom. I wore a navy blue dress. Again, in the church, I was struck by the starkness of the place. No bright flowers or candles. Just a solitary casket draped with a plain church cloth. Richard and Donald cried a lot during the service. I tried very hard to hold it all back. I closed my eyes and listened to the organ music. I let its beautiful tones fill me up like breath in my lungs. This time, it was comforting to have George there beside me. It helped me feel strong, and it gave me a glow inside, allowing me to feel that the future wasn't going to be so bleak. I listened to our minister, Sam Portaro, speaking about all the hurdles my father had overcome and all the suffering he had endured. I had mixed emotions about his death. In some ways, it seemed like a happy celebration because he was back with the only woman he ever loved. Just like he had told her when she slipped away from him in the hospital four years ago, "Until we meet again." But I was very sad too about him being gone. And I was afraid.

I was determined that Richard and Donald and I would get through this, though. We would make our parents proud of us! We would be better than okay. We would be like the Three Musketeers, "One for all and all for one!" I knew in that moment of time that the bond of love between my brothers and me would be what would help us ride out this difficult time. We *would* be okay.

Daddy too was buried in Sunset Cemetery in Christiansburg, right beside my mother. A few days after the funeral service in Williamsburg, we all drove to Christiansburg. It was a beautiful, sunny day, and my Uncle Don spoke for the brief graveside service. We stood at the top of the largest hill where the plot was. The scenery was beautiful, rolling green hills meeting up with blue skies and puffy white clouds. As sad as my brothers and I were, we knew our dad was happier now. Afterward, we returned to my grandmother's house. I didn't even have a chance to change my clothes or relax when my Uncle Don and my Uncle B. asked me to step into the dining room to talk with them alone. They told me to have a seat, and Uncle Don closed the door to the room. The mood was serious and awkward as though they weren't sure of how to proceed. Uncle B. took a seat across from me, but Uncle Don paced as he talked. They took turns speaking very emotionally about promises they made to both my parents about taking care of us. I felt surprised at first. I hadn't thought about the burden of weight they might be carrying. They were concerned about what the three of us were planning for the fall. They knew I wanted to return to Radford to finish that one math class so I could graduate. I would have to leave in about two weeks. Richard was getting ready to begin his freshman year at Virginia Tech at about the same time. That left Donald. My uncles were very unsure about what was best for Donald. He still had three years of high school left, and he didn't want to change schools or move anywhere else. They suggested that it might be better for me not to rush back to Radford so soon, perhaps take a semester off and then go, after we had sorted things out a bit.

That thought petrified me! I wanted my Uncle Don to take Donald to live with them in Suffolk and make Donald feel a part of a real family, but Uncle Don seemed hesitant to embrace that suggestion. He said everyone was worried about Donald not wanting to leave his friends and home. Donald wanted so badly to remain in his current high school.

Also, my grandmother was now living with Uncle Don and Aunt Kay. She never had returned to her old self after her fall at the time of my grandfather's death. She was already a big responsibility for them. I certainly understood that argument. I knew Donald would never want to go live with Uncle B. in Philadelphia, and I really didn't want him to be that far away, either. I felt panicked, sitting there in a closed room with them making me face some very difficult and uncomfortable choices. I felt like I was suffocating. I didn't want them to talk me out of going back to Radford right away. I *had* to come up with a plan for the three and a half months I would be away taking that single math course. I have been blessed with a great deal of stubbornness. It hasn't always been an asset to me, but that day in my life, it sustained me. I was determined to work the situation out. It seemed the only way to get our little family back on the right track. Once I graduated, I could get a teaching position and earn a good salary. The three of us could live together in our house, and I would pay all the bills. I was old enough to be able to take care of Donald while Richard was away at college. I had been taking care of everything, all while Daddy had been at Lake Taylor anyway, I reasoned. I thought of all the family friends who had been so kind and helpful over the last four years. I suddenly brightened at the thought of asking one of them to look after Donald for three months until I could be home for good. My uncles thought it was a long shot, but were willing to allow me a chance to work out the details.

The first person I chose to ask was a close friend of my parents. Mrs. Bruckner had been the one who had driven me home from Radford in May just a few months ago. She had also been the one who had helped us arrange to buy a new car just last summer. She quickly agreed to have Donald stay with her and her family while I was gone to Radford. It would only be until mid-December. Donald could still attend the same high school since she lived only a few miles away from our house. I was ecstatic that I had solved that problem so quickly. I felt empowered. Next, I made a phone call to Radford's off-campus housing office, and with their help, I made arrangements to live in a little house two blocks from campus with three other female students.

Everything seemed to be falling into place. I let my uncles know of the arrangements, and they seemed happy and relieved that I had managed to work everything out so quickly and efficiently. I then went about helping Richard pack for college. He wasn't as enthusiastic about going as I had been when I first started college. I tried to be cheerful and talked about how much fun he would have once he was there. I couldn't help my mind from wandering back to thoughts of Radford. I wanted to recapture the carefree life I had so enjoyed there. Thinking about going back made me feel carefree and lighthearted. I wasn't ready to dwell on the new responsibilities of caring for my brothers and a house with a mortgage full-time just yet. It was an overwhelming reality. I didn't want to admit it, but I was a little afraid of that responsibility. I wanted to be free to do what *I* wanted. And what *I* wanted most right now was to be with George, enjoying our relationship. Over the summer, I had become quite certain that George was the man I would marry. We had taken our relationship slowly and really enjoyed building our friendship. But I couldn't escape the fact that I had come to really love him I sensed that he was feeling the same way I did.

After the Labor Day holiday, I packed Donald off to stay with another family and drove Richard and myself up to the mountains of Virginia. All three of us were filled with anxiety and excitement, but for three different reasons. Donald felt strange having to go live with someone other than family. The Bruckners were collectors of knickknacks, and their house was a bit cluttered. It pained me to think Donald might feel abandoned by Richard and me. I dared not allow myself to dwell on the subject too long. It was just a short time, I kept telling myself. *Three short months, that's all.* Mrs. Bruckner had cleared out her guest room, so Donald had that space all to himself. But most of the other rooms in the house had piles of old newspapers and magazines and stacks of boxes filled with undisclosed treasures. Other than the caring people who lived there, nothing about the house was welcoming. It didn't feel like our home at all. I felt very sad hugging Donald good-bye after helping him settle in. I promised to call him as often as I could.

Helping Richard settle into the dormitory was very different than I had imagined it to be. He was quiet and unenthusiastic, rarely smiling. His mood was so different from what mine had been when I had started as a freshman. We met his roommate, and he seemed to perk up a little bit. I hoped making new friends would help Richard.

I settled into my new routine at Radford with much enthusiasm. The room I rented was in a little house about one block off campus. It was only a ten-minute walk to George's dormitory and a fifteen-minute walk to my math class. I shared the house with two other girls. They were the party type and often were away from the house visiting friends. I too was away from the house a great deal. If I wasn't in class, I was visiting George in his dorm. If George was in class, I would sit in his room and study, or I would visit with his brother, Paul, or other friends who lived on George's hall. I probably should have studied more than I did. I probably should have enlisted the help of an algebra tutor. But I just absorbed everything, every molecule that life had to offer. Because of life insurance money and social security benefits from my parents, I was able to spend money more freely than I ever had before in my life. I indulged myself with clothes and shoes. I often treated my friends to pizza when we studied late into the night. I felt a sense of freedom, a sense of release as I never had before in my life.

The air smelled sweeter. The fall scenery was more beautiful, the colors more vivid. The sunshine felt warmer. I soaked it all up and only allowed my mind to ponder the wonderful bliss of being in love and existing in this bubble of utopia. I never wanted those three months to end. When I had those inevitable moments of having to deal with the reality that was awaiting me at the end of the quarter, I did so quickly, or dodged them entirely. I could tell from my phone conversations with Donald that he was not enjoying his stay with the Bruckners. I always encouraged him to hang in there and make the best of the situation. One time, Mrs. Bruckner complained to me that Donald had dismantled one of her telephones to see how it worked. I was appalled at what he had done, but I also knew that it was typical of Donald to do something like that to satisfy his curiosity. I talked to Richard less often than I did to Donald.

Richard was difficult to coax into long conversations about how he was doing or feeling. Many times I had to leave messages with his roommate since he was in class. Sometimes Richard would call me back, and sometimes he didn't. I assumed Richard was getting into campus life and coming to enjoy life at college. If I had taken off my rose-colored glasses and examined things a bit deeper, I would have realized that all was not right with Richard. He would not tell me until many years later how he suffered from nagging pain and anger over the death of our father. He was depressed and in a dark place, but I didn't realize how he suffered. I didn't know he had taken to running again as he had in high school on the cross-country team. However, at Virginia Tech, my brother ran through dark pastures on the outskirts of campus late at night, past slumbering cows in fields as he fought the angry and painful thoughts, which plagued him constantly. He shouted as he ran, cursing at a God he felt had let him down and abandoned his family. He didn't care whether he lived or died, but I didn't realize he felt that way.

When November rolled around, I was jolted into reality with bitter force as my algebra teacher handed back to me another test paper with a poor grade circled in red ink at the top.

I allowed my success in that math class to get away from me. I realized that I probably wasn't going to pass the class unless some miracle happened. Pro-and-con arguments battled each other in my head. *Should I admit to biting off more than I could chew and drop the class now?* That would mean admitting it to more than just myself. It would also mean leaving George sooner than I had planned. Just the thought of having to do that was too much for me. George was the one person I could count on. He made me feel like I could do *anything.* My plan to finish the class and graduate so I could properly care for my brothers just *had* to work out. I decided to try studying harder and make every effort to pass the class. I only had to get a D, for heaven sake, I reasoned to myself. But what I found was that when you don't understand the material, more studying isn't much help. I became more confused than ever. George's brother, Paul, tried to help me out and tutor me a bit. I could do the complicated steps of the problems when Paul was at my side, reminding me what to do. But on my own in class, it was a different story. I had a great deal of difficulty concentrating, and I had no confidence in myself to remember what to do to solve the problems. As the days wore on toward Thanksgiving, I began to quietly prepare myself for the possibility of my plan not working out as I had hoped. George was having some difficulty in his English class, and I much preferred helping him to studying math. English was my favorite subject, and I excelled in it. It was like second nature to me, unlike the complicated algebra problems, which seemed to lack purpose and reason, in my opinion. I often joked with Paul and George, saying, "Who really cares what X is?"

In hindsight, I know that I expected too much from myself. I had hardly allowed myself to grieve for the loss of my father; and there I was, trying to pass a class, which required a lot of concentration and effort that I was not emotionally ready to give. I had run away from all the impending responsibilities at home and had sought sanctuary in my college campus in the company of my friends and George. As they say, all good things must come to an end. I failed the math course at the end of the quarter, and I went home to Williamsburg for the Christmas holidays with a new plan in mind.

Donald moved back into our house with me and was happier than I'd seen him in a long time. He was glad his time away from home was over. Despite the Christmas season, Richard was somber and moody. He was having a hard time adjusting to our new life without parents, but he wouldn't talk much about his feelings. We had a quiet Christmas celebration, spending much of it in Suffolk with Uncle Don and Aunt Kay.

After Christmas, I was officially made Donald's legal guardian. Richard had turned eighteen back in September, so he didn't need a legal guardian. At just twenty-two, I was going to be legally responsible for a soon-to-be sixteen-year-old. That was a bit scary! All of the responsibilities at home and the legalities of it all scared me a little, but I didn't want to admit that to myself, much less to anyone else. I had virtually run off to Radford to get away from the oppression of it all. I wasn't happy or proud of how that choice had turned out. I refused to give up, though. I would have to try again. I knew it was out of the question to try to return to Radford just yet. I hoped that somehow I could go back again in a few semesters, but it was too soon just now. Donald needed me, and I couldn't imagine asking him to go live with someone else again so I could return to Radford. I decided to explore the possibilities of taking the course at a college closer to home and having the grade transferred. I also needed to find a job. A friend at our church ran a well-known preschool in Williamsburg. I interviewed for a job with her and was hired there to assist with the three-year-olds' class. I really enjoyed my job at Greenwood Preschool, and happily, it provided me with teaching experience. I knew that would be a plus once I finally graduated.

Our house had been neglected for sometime with Daddy's illness keeping him from doing much upkeep. I started redecorating a bit. A little fresh paint here and there helped a lot. I bought new lamps for the living room and made new curtains for the dining room. With George's help during spring break, I added chair rails with wallpaper below in the dining room too. I moved from my old bedroom back to what had been my parents' bedroom. New curtains and bedspread made the room more my own, and being in that room gave me comfort as though my parents were right there with me. I gave my old room to Donald. It was bigger than his, and he was excited to have a new space. Time moved more quickly than I ever imagined it could. Before I knew it, summer was upon us, and Richard was home from college. Richard had a friend who needed a place for the summer, so we rented our guest room to him. It felt odd having a new face living in our house. Richard worked long hours at his summer job and didn't hang around the house much. Donald and I kept the grass mowed and tended the flowerbeds, trying to make everything look neat. George visited quite often and helped around the house as well. Now on my trips to take out the trash, I noticed *two* doves residing in the pine tree in our side yard.

CHAPTER TWELVE

Just as I began to really enjoy the hustle and bustle of having extra people in and out of my home, summer came to a close. Richard and his friend headed back to college. George did too. The house seemed lonely with the quiet that surrounded me. This was Donald's junior year in high school. He ventured out with friends more than he had in the past. I found that I suddenly had a lot of extra time on my hands. It felt like it was time to tie up my loose ends. I needed to finally graduate.

My friend Lou Ann told me that another friend of ours, Heidi, was taking classes at Christopher Newport College in the evenings. Lou Ann suggested I call Heidi and go with her to sign up for my class when she registered for hers. I liked the idea of having a friend with me, so I called Heidi about it. Heidi proved to be a truer friend than I ever imagined. She did better than just go with me. She signed up for the same class and offered to do the homework and study together! Now I was very busy. I taught until noon and then went to class in the evenings. In between, I cleaned the house, fixed meals, paid bills, helped Donald with his homework, and studied for my own class. I started working out three times a week at a local women's fitness center. I felt good about myself and the path I was on, but the math class still proved to be difficult for me.

I would complain to Heidi, saying my brain just wasn't wired to understand this type of math.

She remained positive and supportive of me. She was my personal cheerleader, and she encouraged me to work harder and not to give up. I maintained a weak C grade throughout most of the class. As exam time drew nearer, I began to panic. It was going to be a cumulative exam, and I was worried about being able to remember all the material the class had covered in the semester and apply it on this one test. The exam was tough, and the days leading up to getting my final grade in the mail were stressful. I had so much anxiety about how I had done and whether I had passed the exam. When I finally received the envelope in the mailbox, I opened it with trembling fingers. I could feel the thumping of my heartbeat in my chest. The printing swam before my eyes. I scanned down to the end of the page . . . I passed!

I had not applied for graduation at Radford before taking the math course. I wanted to wait and make sure I passed the course first. Now that I had passed, I sent my new transcripts from the class along with my application to graduate in the spring. I felt such a sense of accomplishment.

Everything was finally falling into place even if it was a bit later than I had first imagined.

In late February, I received in the mail a letter of acceptance for graduation. I was so excited. I immediately called to tell George. We planned a weekend trip for me to come to Radford to visit him, and while I was there, I could order my cap and gown. Donald had just celebrated his seventeenth birthday. I felt guilty, leaving him home alone, but he seemed happy to stay by himself for the weekend. It would, he reminded me, only be three days, as I was leaving on Friday and would return home by Sunday. I hugged him good-bye Friday morning as he left for the school bus and made him promise to call me if he needed anything. The five-hour drive flew by faster than I had ever experienced. I was so anxious to see George. Our relationship had grown and matured quite a lot over the last year. We had discussed the possibility of getting married and spending our lives together as soon as he graduated in two more years.

The weekend with George was blissful. I reluctantly opened by eyes to the morning light on Sunday, knowing I would have to say good-bye and drive back home in a few hours. George and I went to brunch, lingering at the restaurant as long as we could. When we returned to his dorm room around noon, his suite mate told us we had just missed a phone call from my neighbor at home, Emily Richardson.

I felt a jab of panic. *Why in the world would she be calling me here?* I wondered. *Had something happened to Donald?* I dialed her number. She answered after only two rings. Her voice was calm and steady as she spoke, but I could hear the concern in her tone.

"Elizabeth, I am sorry to have to call you there, but something has happened. Donald is okay, but there has been a fire at your house." A little fireworks display began exploding immediately inside my head. I sat down on the bed beside me. "Oh no," I whispered.

"Listen, it's not that bad," she reassured me. "Most of the damage is in Donald's bedroom. He was very quick acting! He used the garden hose outside his window to try to put the fire out. The fire crew has left now, and Donald is across the street here with me at my house."

"Thank you so much," I whispered in response as my voice seemed to catch in my throat. She continued on, "We called your uncle in Suffolk, but no one answered. I recall that he is a pastor, so I guess he is still at church right now. We will keep trying to reach him for you."

"Okay," I answered. "Thank you for calling me and caring for Donald. I'll leave here soon and be home before dinnertime," I told her. I felt numb. What could I expect when I finally arrived back home? What about all the redecorating I had done? I was extremely grateful that Donald was all right. *Thank you, God, but how much more can we take?* I wondered as I hung up the telephone. I explained everything to George. He was in disbelief. I wished so much that he could come to Williamsburg with me, but I knew it wasn't possible. He needed to stay at college. He shouldn't miss his classes.

If the ride to Radford had seemed extremely fast, the ride back home two days later seemed twice as long in comparison. I hardly remembered much of the trip as my mind was so lost in thoughts of what to expect when I would finally pull into my driveway. I arrived in the late afternoon. My Uncle Don was standing outside the house, talking to Donald and Emily Richardson. I turned off the car and ran up to Donald, pulling him into a big hug. Tears filled my eyes. "I'm so glad you are okay!" I kept saying to him. He seemed a bit numb, not talking too much, but he gave me his familiar smile. Uncle Don hugged me. "You must brace yourself, Lizzy," he said. "There is a lot of smoke damage throughout the house. We are so lucky that it never got up in the attic."

I looked over at the house for the first time. Blackened areas of soot surrounded the opening to what had been Donald's window. The window glass was broken. Furniture from his room was strewn about the grass in the side yard between our next-door neighbors. I noticed only the bed seemed to be missing. The rest of the house seemed the same. "How did this happen?" I asked. Uncle Don spoke more quietly as he answered as though he only wanted me to hear him. "It looks like Donald forgot to blow out a candle he had lit in his room. The firemen surmised that the curtains next to his desk caught first and ignited the bed next. The bed was totally destroyed. Donald says he heard the roar and crackle of the flames from the kitchen where he was making something to eat. He ran down the hall toward his room, but the fire was getting too big. He ran back to the kitchen and dialed 911, and then he ran outside to the garden hose and broke the window to spray water on the fire inside. One fireman told Mrs. Richardson that if Donald had not used the hose, the fire would have exploded into the attic, and there would have been no saving the house after that."

Uncle Don had been telling me all this as we walked up to the house. Now we were standing at the front door. The glass in the storm door had a dark film all over it from the smoke. The strong odor of the soot filled my nostrils. We opened the door and went inside.

"Ohh!" I sucked air into my lungs quickly as I scanned the room. The ceiling and the walls from the ceiling to about midway down were blackened. You couldn't even tell that I had recently painted the room. The new curtains in the dining room were blackened and ruined. A heavy, sooty dust had settled over all the furniture and everything sitting about. We walked down the hallway. Here, the walls were so dark with soot it seemed like nighttime. Richard's room was next to Donald's. Plastic models of the *Star Wars* spaceships had melted as they stood on a shelf. Water mixed with soot had left streaks down the blue walls of the room, and the paint itself had bubbled up in some places on the wall closest to Donald's room. The plastic-coated window shade had melted some, causing it to scrunch and curl up. The heat from the fire in the next room must have been incredible. Donald's room was unrecognizable. The walls beside the window were burned through to the studs.

The room was like an empty, blistered shell. It was a very sad sight to behold. Next, we walked back toward my bedroom. Though the soot wasn't as thick in that area, it was still on everything. The wallpaper in the master bath looked ruined. It had streaks of black soot all over it. The new white curtains I had enjoyed so much now were gray. They had torn on their own as the heat had apparently destroyed the seams holding them together. They hung in shreds from the rods, looking pitiful. Soot was everywhere! Even in the walk-in closet where my clothes hung behind closed doors. The whole house felt dirty and dismal. I felt a huge sensation of defeat. "All my hard work! All the redecorating I did is ruined," I whispered. Uncle Don patted me on the back. "Insurance will cover it all, I expect. The most important thing is that Donald is alive and safe." I knew he was right. Things can be replaced, but not people you love. I squared my shoulders. I certainly could redecorate all over again. I had fun doing it the first time. It would be fun to do it a second time too.

The next couple months were a blur of activity. Donald and I had to move into a motel suite since the house wasn't livable during all the renovation to repair the fire damage. Our insurance representative was extremely helpful to us and aided us in putting the pieces of our lives back together. I had to pick out new paint colors, wallpaper, and light fixtures for the builders. Donald had lost just about all his belongings in the fire except for a few things we were able to retrieve from his dresser drawers. In addition to buying him new clothes and shoes, he needed a new bed, nightstand, dresser, and desk. None of his old furniture was salvageable due to the intense heat from the fire. I also had to buy him new beddings and curtains. Most of the rooms needed new curtains, and everything that didn't need to be replaced needed to be dry-cleaned to remove the soot. In fact, all my clothes from my closet, as well as all the towels and sheets from the linen closet, had to be sent to the dry cleaners. Our insurance agent arranged for a local dry cleaner to send over a truck one morning to pick up all the items needing to be cleaned. Two weeks later, everything was ready. Members of our church arranged for us to store the cleaned items in a vacant Sunday-school classroom until our house was ready. The truck met me at the church to deliver all the neatly folded or hung items. The driver and I made several trips into the building to store all the items in the classroom.

At times I became very overwhelmed by the scope and magnitude of all that we owned in the house, what was lost, and what had to be replaced. These were not the typical kinds of things an average twenty-three-year-old would deal with and worry about. Many nights I cried myself to sleep. The two months it took to renovate the house seemed to drag on endlessly. It was the end of April before we moved back into our home. It smelled like fresh paint instead of soot. It felt like the house had been through a deep cleansing. My thoughts turned to my upcoming graduation ceremony at Radford in a few weeks. *A fresh start for everything*, I surmised to myself, smiling.

CHAPTER THIRTEEN

The spring weather was perfect the weekend of my graduation, with cloudless blue skies and sun-drenched, seventy-five-degree days. I arrived in town two days early so I could spend some time with George. Many students were packing up and heading for home. But the graduating seniors were milling about campus, spending time with family members and visiting with each other. There was an excited feeling in the air. George was particularly happy and upbeat the day I arrived. He kept telling me how proud he was of me, but at the same time, he seemed preoccupied with something. We had lunch together at the home of his adopted grandmother, Ms. Blanche. The local Methodist church had a campus program where, in the fall, they paired older church members together with college students. It benefited both the students and the senior citizens, creating support and friendships.

Ms. Blanche had taken a shine to George right away, and she had come to treat him as good as any real grandmother would. She had never married in her life but had taught in the elementary school in the area for over forty years before retiring. She was well known and well loved in the Radford community and was a big alumni supporter. She was also very active in the Methodist church where George now attended, and he would escort her to Sunday services each week. Ms. Blanche served us a delicious lunch of chicken salad and fresh fruit, with her special lemon squares for dessert. After eating, we spent some time chatting with her in her garden, and we admired her tall golden yellow bearded iris. They were her favorite flower, and she was very proud of the large number she had, growing in her patio garden. She reminisced about her teaching career and told me all about what I might expect when I began teaching too. It was midafternoon when we left her company and returned to George's dormitory. The second floor where he lived felt deserted, but we heard quiet talking and an occasional giggle coming from the suite directly across from his room. George became somewhat agitated as we entered his room, but no one else was there, and I couldn't figure out whether something was bothering him or not. He seemed very happy, smiling a lot, but I still had the feeling he was preoccupied. I tried to question him about it, but he attempted to divert my attention with small talk. Then two of the girls from across the hall popped their heads in the doorway and greeted us, wishing me well on my graduation. A few minutes later, George's suitemates returned to their room, and the quiet time we had been enjoying seemed to evaporate. George suddenly hopped up from where he was sitting and grabbed his half-full laundry basket, mumbling something about needing to do a load of wash. I shook my head, confused, as I watched him duck quickly out of the door. I didn't follow him. The laundry room was down at the other end of his hallway, and it would be five minutes or so before he returned. I turned on his television and clicked through a few channels. Again, one of the girls from across the hall stuck her head in the doorway.

"George is calling for you to come down to the laundry room," she told me.

"Okay," I said. After turning off the TV set, I wandered down to where he was. The laundry room was very large. The humidity and heat from the spinning dryers immediately engulfed me as I entered the room. With no curtains or blinds, the room was very bright, and sunlight bounced off the yellow-tiled walls. George looked up as I entered and walked over to him. He managed a weak smile. I sensed some trepidation in his eyes. I looked back at him, a puzzled expression on my face. With a sudden movement, he grabbed my hand and pulled from his pocket a small black satin box. Immediate recognition of what he was about to do flashed into my mind, but I surprised myself by hesitating and attempting to pull my hand away from his grasp.

"Oh, George," I whispered, "not in here!"

My eyes flashed around the stark room. It was a very unromantic place, not at all how I had imagined something like this happening to me. As soon as the words left my mouth, I regretted uttering them. *What if I have ruined everything?* I thought wildly to myself. George persevered as though I had not said a word. He tightened his grasp on my hand and took a deep breath. He wore a very determined look. I fastened my eyes on his face. I wasn't going to let anything take away from this moment. "I think you know how I feel about you," he was saying. His lips continued to move, but I suddenly couldn't hear the words. I was floating, swimming in bliss.

His hands trembled as he opened the box, fumbling a bit. Inside, lying on an ivory satin pillow, was a beautiful diamond ring. Its large round stone winked at me in the bright sunlight. I gasped as my mouth formed an O shape, but no words came. George took the ring from the box and slipped it on my finger. "Will you marry me?" he asked. The silence broke. A joyous, breathless laugh gurgled up from my throat, and I grabbed his neck in a tight hug. "Yes, oh yes, of course, I will," I answered. He kissed me and then looked into my eyes. A huge grin spread across his face, brighter than any sunlight in the room. "I'm sorry, but I couldn't wait any longer. I've been trying to figure out a good time and place since you got here. I have been so excited I just couldn't stand it any longer! I have wanted to tell you about it for weeks!"

He held my hand up so the facets caught the sunlight from the window, and a hundred little sparkling circles of light danced across the nearby wall. "I wish it could have been bigger," he said, staring wistfully at the ring. I was shocked. "Oh no, George!" I said immediately. "It's perfect. I love it just as it is. It is plenty big." I stared at the glittering jewel on my finger. "We certainly have good news to tell everyone at graduation on Saturday."

The day of graduation dawned with picture-perfect weather. My best friend, Adaline, and another good friend, Pam, as well as my Uncle Don, arrived for the ceremony. They were all pleased about the good news George and I shared with them. While it seemed a little strange to be standing in a line of hundreds of graduates, all of whom I didn't know, I didn't let that lonely feeling take hold of me. I was beaming with happiness, and I felt so proud of myself. I felt incredibly blessed to be graduating and also to be getting married sometime soon. I knew my parents would be so proud, especially Momma, who had always regarded education as vitally important.

When I walked across the outdoor platform, in front of the college library, in my black cap and gown, I felt like a regal princess. As I accepted my diploma, for a fleeting moment, I looked out over the green lawns of the campus and the brick buildings where I had taken so many classes and learned so much. I was finally closing this chapter of my life.

CHAPTER FOURTEEN

When I returned home from my graduation, I began to send out teaching job applications for school districts in the Williamsburg area. Deep down I hoped to become employed with York County Public Schools and teach at my old elementary school. The building was located just a mile from our house, and I liked the feeling of being able to give back to the community that had helped me so much over the years. I still had my job at Greenwood Preschool to fall back on if no districts hired me right away, but I was very anxious to start a public school teaching career and acquire benefits that would help our family. Donald was starting his senior year in the fall. He hadn't talked much about where he might want to attend college. I wanted him to go, of course, but I wondered if he was really ready for the responsibilities that came along with it.

My run of good fortune continued. In late August, I received a phone call from the principal of my old elementary school. She offered me a first-grade teaching position. I was ecstatic, and I accepted the offer without hesitation. It turned out to be a perfect first teaching job. I worked with a caring team of teachers; some of them had been at the school for a number of years and had taught my brothers. It felt like a family, and it was just what I needed to boost my confidence and guide me along as a new teacher.

Donald began working after school and weekends at a specialty shop located in the downtown Williamsburg area. He enjoyed making money, and he had made some very good friends at the shop. He rarely studied much, but managed to maintain a pretty decent grade average. He was so smart. He could rattle off facts about events in history that most people didn't remember. He just wasn't interested in school. He didn't care about sports or extracurricular activities. He hated taking tests. He always said, "Why do I have to take a test to prove what I know when I already know it?"

I realized that Donald wasn't ready to go away to college long before he began talking to me about it. He decided to take a year off after graduating from high school and just work and save some money. He was conflicted about what he would major in should he attend college in the future. He wanted to explore some options and take his time in deciding.

The following spring, Richard graduated from Virginia Tech with a degree in mechanical engineering. It was one of the proudest days of my life. That summer was filled with planning the last-minute details of my wedding. On a sultry, hot day in late August of 1987, I married George Armstrong. The ceremony was held at Bruton Parish Church amid the bursting fuchsia blooms of the crepe myrtle trees in the historic area. My Uncle B. walked me down the aisle. My Uncle Don helped officiate during the ceremony. George had arranged to have bouquets of daisies and roses placed on the seats in the church where my parents would have sat. It was as perfect an event as I ever dreamed it would be.

Having changed his major, George didn't graduate until the spring of 1988. We lived a year in Radford, and I taught second grade there. Richard and Donald had moved into an apartment together in Williamsburg. Donald had decided to study history and get a liberal arts degree. He continued to work days and took a couple classes in the evenings at a nearby community college.

Richard had begun working at the Norfolk shipyard in their engineering department. His commute was about forty-five minutes one way. I wasn't happy about my brothers renting an apartment at first. Our house was left sitting with no one living in it. George helped me realize that Richard and Donald needed to move on. The house overwhelmed them with its required upkeep and memories of what had been. After George graduated, we moved back to Williamsburg and lived in the house. Our goal was to clean it out and get it ready to put on the market. George accepted a job offer from an insurance company in Richmond. He planned to commute to Richmond each day to work until we were able to sell the house. That summer was long and difficult for me.

Our house had been a safe haven and a symbol of the love and security given us by our parents. I found it extremely painful to go through everything in the house and decide to keep it or throw it out or give it away. George would often get frustrated with me at my indecision about what to do with some items. He kept telling me that giving up an object doesn't mean giving away the memory. Memories are something no one can take from you. It is yours forever. I knew he was right, but after all I had been through and all I had lost, certain objects came to represent the people I wasn't able to replace. I couldn't bear to part with my mother's black coat with the fur collar or her bottle of perfume or her collection of English teacups and saucers. There was no question that I would hang on to Daddy's record collection, his train set, and all his tools. We easily divided the furniture and Christmas ornaments amongst the three of us. The things we weren't sure about or ready to make a decision on, we decided to store at a local storage unit establishment. By the end of June, we had the house on the market, but the company we first chose to list it wasn't very aggressive. There were few showings, and I began to get very downhearted about the lack of progress. The long commute to Richmond was draining for George, but he rarely complained about it.

Around the first of August, we decided to switch to a new realtor company to list the house. They presented a well-thought-out plan for selling our house, and almost immediately after signing with them, the house showings began. By the end of the month, we had a decent offer for the house, and we accepted it. Closing was set for the third week in September, and by October 1, we moved to the south side of Richmond. We rented a two-story colonial-style townhouse. I had applied for teaching positions in the Richmond area, but had not been offered one. I applied to be an assistant director at a childcare center near our new home and was hired. I knew it would be a temporary job for the remainder of the year. Moving to Richmond was a bit unsettling for me at first. I had a lot of bad memories associated with Richmond because it was where much of my mother's suffering had taken place in her battle against cancer.

Despite my reservations, I loved the little townhouse; and the first morning in my new home, I awoke to the familiar sound of cooing doves. I knew everything would be okay.

A year later, I was hired as a first-grade teacher for a small district twenty minutes outside of Richmond. George and I began house hunting, and in October, we found the perfect home. We bought it and moved in by Christmas. I heard the cooing of the doves outside my bedroom window not too long after moving in there. It suddenly struck me that this couldn't be a coincidence. I always liked entertaining the idea that the doves were following me, but it had been more of wishful thinking. Yet it kept happening! I felt deep down that it was happening for a reason. It was a sign that I was on the right path and had blessings from above.

By the end of June, we found out I was pregnant. George and I couldn't have been happier!

On January 16, 1991, we welcomed Katherine Elizabeth Armstrong into the family. She was five weeks premature, but otherwise healthy, and we were able to bring her home from the hospital right away. Not long after our Katie was born, my brother Richard began seriously dating a very special girl, Susan. Donald was continuing to take a few classes and had taken on a second job as an interpreter for the Colonial Williamsburg Foundation. He loved dressing in costume and entertaining the visitors. Eventually, Donald got a full-time position as an interpreter at the Jamestown Fort, a recreated village of the original. He thrived there and made many new friends. His work there helped him realize he wanted to be a curator of a museum someday. He also liked teaching the school groups that visited about history and the way life was at the time. He had a gift for connecting with his audience when he interpreted. He knew what to say and what to do to make the history come alive for his listeners. He began writing a book about weaponry used at the time Jamestown Fort was built.

Four years after Katie was born, George and I welcomed another child into our lives. This time it was a son, Nicholas Jordan Armstrong. Not long after Nick was born, Richard married Susan and bought a home in Williamsburg. Donald traveled to England to study abroad for a year in London at Middlesex University. He was only a few classes short of graduating, but he couldn't pass up such a fantastic opportunity to go study in the country of our ancestors, a place he had always dreamed of visiting.

It turned out to be the most fantastic year of Donald's life. He vowed that he would return to England to live there someday. He went back to interpreting at Jamestown and finished his degree, graduating the following spring. He had taken many more years than Richard or I to graduate, but he had taken it slowly and had grown up a lot along the way. He finished writing his book and searched for a publisher. Because of his connections working for Jamestown, he easily found a publisher who specialized in historically accurate works. The thrill he had at becoming a published author was contagious. He grinned from ear to ear all the time. He was becoming well known in historical circles. Entitled *Soldiers of the Virginia Colony, 1607-1699*, his book was cited as the best example of a historical work on colonial weaponry thus far. He was recognized outside of Virginia as well, and it wasn't long before a new job opportunity presented itself to him. He had the chance to become the director of a small outdoor-living museum in Maryland situated along the Potomac River. Moving away from the only town he had ever lived in was a huge step for Donald. Aside from studying in London for a year, he had never lived anywhere else. Richard and I had always looked out for our younger brother. But this was a good opportunity for Donald. He felt like he was stagnating in Williamsburg, and his job in Jamestown wasn't leading anywhere.

At about this same time, George and I prepared our family for a move as well. George too felt like he needed to move on in his career. A new management position had opened for him, but it meant our moving to Knoxville, Tennessee. I was petrified at the thought of moving. I had lived in different towns in Virginia, but never in another state. The unknown frightened me a great deal. I hated selling our first home. We had put so much into decorating and landscaping it, and it was a loving, secure place. It was where we had brought both our children home from the hospital. I was also very worried about living farther away from my brothers. It meant we couldn't see each other as often, and now Richard and Susan were expecting their first baby. But George considered it an adventure. He did his best to reassure me and make the move easier for me. The day we left was extremely sad for me. I cried on and off throughout the long drive. I kept thinking to myself, *God, please let everything turn out okay. Please help me like this new life. Please take care of Richard and Donald for me.*

As we passed over the state line between Virginia and Tennessee, I noticed a rainbow. I smiled, and the beautiful colors cheered me a bit. It disappeared. We drove on, and a few minutes later, another one arched across the sky. I began to feel an excitement boil up inside me. Katie pointed at the back window, "Look, Mommy, another rainbow is back here." Sure enough, a third rainbow stretched out in the sky behind us. We kept watching, and before the trip to our new hometown was over, we counted seven separate rainbows! "This has to be a sign!" I told George. "Someone up there is trying to tell me to stop crying because everything is going to work out and be fine!"

And it was—right down to the two doves that stood on our roof each morning and each evening and sung to us.

CHAPTER FIFTEEN

It was within the first few months of living in Knoxville that I decided to begin writing this story. It had always been waiting for me in the back of my mind, a little seed waiting for the right time to grow. I didn't get a teaching position right away, so I filled my extra time with writing at the computer while Katie was at school and Nicholas napped. I was surprised at how the words flowed as my fingers raced across the computer keys. The memories flooded back, clearly and vividly as if they had just happened. I found myself laughing at funny remembrances and crying uncontrollably at others. Parts of this story were very difficult to write, and other pieces seemed to write themselves. By the time we moved again five years later, I felt certain I had fully completed this story to the best of my ability.

This move brought our family to Columbus, Ohio. Columbus is the home office location of the company George works for and a place he had dreamed of coming to work. He loved the idea of an office high up on a twenty-something floor, being in the hub of where all the great ideas were born and then executed. I handled this move better than I had the last. This time I knew what to expect, and I knew we would manage to make a good life in this new city, just as we had before. We decided to rent a large townhouse and get to know the area before deciding to buy a new home. Both our children were of school age, and a good school system was vitally important to us. It was only a few days after we moved in that I began to see doves. They seemed to be everywhere! I would see them on the telephone wires, or at the bird feeder in the yard next to ours. One would constantly perch on the ledge outside our bedroom window and coo soothingly.

The hardest thing about this move was being even farther away from my brothers. Richard and Susan had just welcomed a new daughter into their family, and I had not even had a chance to see her yet. Donald had hit a rough patch in the previous year. He had met with a lot of discontent from some of his coworkers at the Maryland museum. Donald had come into that job with a lot of new ideas about how the museum could be run more effectively, but others there wanted the old ways to remain. Donald had turned to teaching history part-time at a small college near where he lived. He found that he loved teaching and wished in hindsight that he had pursued a teaching certificate before he had graduated so he could teach history at the high school level. Now he didn't feel he had the time or money to afford that certification. Donald loved teaching as much as he came to dislike his museum job. He was torn about what to do because the teaching job he had didn't pay as much as he needed. Finally, he couldn't compromise his principles any longer, and he resigned from the museum position. He called me often for advice and comfort. I wasn't as much help to him as I thought I should have been. I felt rather helpless being so far away. I was a bit discouraged myself over having difficulty in finding a teaching position in Columbus. But I did my best to encourage Donald to continue teaching and at the same time look for something else. That was no easy feat, considering he lived in a very rural part of Maryland. His car was old and not too reliable. He was worried about the possibility of having to commute a lengthy distance. I finally told him that he would *have* to make some kind of drastic change. If he needed to move somewhere else to find a good job, then we would help him. George suggested that Donald look into getting a job in the insurance field. It had been successful for George, and there were plenty of opportunities for someone just starting out. Donald respected George's opinion a lot and decided to explore his suggestion.

We were well into fall by this time. Donald continued to call me two or three times a week to talk and to ask for my advice. We had lengthy conversations about how much we missed each other and reminisced about things we had been through together in the past. Always the optimist, I tried to be encouraging and supportive. Many times he was depressed and felt his life was going nowhere. We talked about life and death and how we missed Momma and Daddy. I reminded Donald about the doves and how they helped me feel encouraged at my lowest times. He chuckled sarcastically and said, "Liz, those doves only seem to be sent to you. I wish I would get a few of those doves sent my way. Heck, all I ever see are buzzards!"

We got a good laugh out of that one. It became a running joke between the two of us when we talked. Laughter is always a good medicine when you feel down. Just before Halloween, Donald called me with wonderful news. He had an interview in Roanoke, Virginia, for a position as an insurance claims adjuster. He was so excited. He had made arrangements to drive there with Uncle Don, and Uncle Don had already helped him go out and buy a new suit for the interview. It had been a long time since I had heard such joy and promise in Donald's voice on the phone. I told him how proud I was of him, and I went out the next day and bought him a funny Halloween card. I slipped a twenty-dollar bill inside with a note saying to spend it on something fun, and then I put it in the mail.

Donald didn't call again for several days. He had started writing a new book, and since leaving his museum job, he had spent a lot of time writing. I was fairly busy myself. I had started working part-time at a small private school across the street from our townhouse complex. They needed someone to teach art classes twice a week, and since it was a foot in the door, I gladly accepted. With that and two children and Halloween activities, I had plenty to do.

On a Saturday, two days after Halloween, George and I took the children on a fun afternoon of exploring. We had heard about a great Amish furniture store and restaurant about fifteen miles away. We were in need of a hallway table, so we decided to find this place that so many people raved about. It turned out to be a very successful trip. We found the perfect table and ate a delicious home-style lunch. We arrived home after five o'clock. George checked the mail, and I fed the cat. The children chatted happily about all the fun they'd had. I turned on a few lights, filling the kitchen area with a warm glow as the evening light began to fade outside. George handed me a letter from the stack of mail he had retrieved. It was a letter from Uncle B. "Oh good!" I said and reached across the countertop for a letter opener sitting beside the telephone. The phone suddenly rang, startling me. "I'll bet that's Donald," I said, smiling. We hadn't talked since two days before Halloween, and I had anticipated a call from him sometime over the weekend. I picked it up.

"Hello?" I answered. A frantic voice called out my name on the other end of the line. "Liz!"

It felt like a bucket of icy cold water had been poured over me. A feeling of dread engulfed me. Although he had only said my name, the panicked tone in Richard's voice was all too familiar.

Something inside me whispered, "Brace yourself."

Richard's voice was breathless, distressed, and his words came quickly. "Liz, I hope you are sitting down. I have the worst news ever! It's bad . . . it's really bad!" In the fleeting seconds it took Richard to speak, I pictured dozens of different scenarios flashing across my mind like a movie preview on fast-forward. I took a deep breath. A practiced calm descended over me. "What happened?" I asked. His answer was not something I expected.

"It's Donald . . . he died. Donald is dead, Liz. He's dead!" His last sentence was more of a squeak as he lost control. I was silent. I felt a prickling at the back of my eye sockets. I resisted it. I closed my eyes, trying to take in the words I had heard, but they hung from the rafters of my brain like a heavy smoke, clouding my thinking. I took a deep breath. "How?" I asked. "What happened?" I opened my eyes. George was standing in front of me, a look of concerned curiosity on his face. He mouthed to me, "What's wrong?" I grabbed a notepad and pencil we always kept near the phone and jotted down, *Donald died.*

George's face crumpled as he read my scribbled response. I looked away. I had to be strong. I focused my eyes on the pebbled pattern of the countertop. Richard had composed himself again.

"It happened about an hour ago," he was saying. "Donald had some kind of seizure. He just collapsed." This seemed strange. Donald was never sick. "Where was he?" I interjected.

"He was at the market near his apartment, in the deli section. He was ordering some meat, and then he collapsed. There were two people there who knew CPR. They started working on him, and then the paramedics arrived quickly. They said he was convulsing, and it was an unusually long seizure . . . over four minutes. He got really red in the face, and then he came around for about a minute. He was able to give his name and address. Then he grabbed his chest and said he couldn't breathe. Then he collapsed again. They rushed him to the hospital. The doctors worked on him for a while. They told me they did everything they could, but he was gone. They couldn't bring him back. They said a blood clot went to his lung. That's why he couldn't breathe."

Richard was crying again. I realized I was gripping the phone so tightly that my fingers were going numb. My ear felt sore from the pressure of the receiver next to it. I could find no words for the moment. It all seemed so unreal, and yet it had happened, and no amount of wishing or praying or crying would change any of it. I felt an incredible sadness that Donald had endured this horrible event alone. I wished I could have been there to hold his hand, to say good-bye, to tell him I loved him beyond measure.

Weight issues had plagued much of Donald's life. Having to deal with the uncertainty of parental illness from a very young age, Donald had learned to use food for comfort. As an adult, he had achieved significant weight loss since returning from London. But the job difficulties in the past year had overwhelmed him, and he had put much of the weight back on. I know the difficulties of weight loss myself, and I never chastised Donald. I only encouraged him and supported him. I worried that someday he might face heart problems, but he was thirty-four. I had never expected something like this now.

"He is in a better place now," I told Richard. "He is happy, and he is back with Momma and Daddy. Our sadness is really for ourselves because we miss him so, but I know he is happier than we can ever imagine."

Richard sniffed. "I know," he answered quietly. "We have a lot of plans to make," I told him.

"Yes," he agreed. "There will be an autopsy. And there is something else. Donald had signed his organ donation card on the back of his license. We have to let the hospital know if we choose to honor it or not." I did not even hesitate. "Why wouldn't we?" I asked. "Donald wouldn't have signed it if it wasn't something he wanted. I am sure it was important to him. Anyway, it will be a positive in all this."

"Okay," Richard agreed. "It is just a formality. I'll call the hospital back and let them know. There is a limited time frame for harvesting organs."

CHAPTER SIXTEEN

George and I made arrangements to leave for Williamsburg the next morning. It was a long nine-hour drive. The children handled the trip well. They read books or napped most of the way. I was very quiet and reflective throughout the trip. I watched the sky for signs, but no rainbows appeared. I couldn't help but wonder why I hadn't sensed that something was wrong. Donald and I had been so close. Why hadn't I known somehow that he was slipping away from this world? I had a legal pad on my lap, and I twirled an ink pen in my fingers. I had started lists of things Richard and I had to accomplish in the next twenty-four hours. I had written names of pallbearers and others to call. I had also started writing a piece to be put into the local papers, as well as words I wanted to speak at his funeral. Donald's funeral would be held at Bruton Parish Church, but I wanted it to be different from Momma's and Daddy's. Theirs had been stiffly formal. Donald's, I felt, should be more friendly, just as he had been. Richard and I had discussed it, and it was important to both of us to address the crowd that came to gather at his funeral. Both of us had important things to say about our brother.

Richard had made arrangements for us to stay at a local hotel not too far from where he lived. During the day, we spent most of our time in his home. Word about Donald's sudden death had spread quickly, and many friends came to pay their respects and bring food. Once the obituary appeared in the paper, it seemed the phone never stopped ringing. We heard from people we didn't even remember. One of Donald's former grammar school teachers called to say how sorry she was and to share some funny anecdotes about the little boy she had taught so long ago. Potted plants and flower bouquets were delivered several times throughout the day. Richard and I met with the new minister of Bruton and the organist, who had been a family friend for years. Donald had left no will, no funeral arrangements. Richard and I did the best we could to choose songs and prayers we thought would have pleased our brother. At the funeral home, we decided on a simple casket of polished oak. Donald's body had been delayed in being sent to the Williamsburg funeral home due to the harvesting of organs at the Maryland hospital. They weren't even sure if it would arrive in time for the visitation night. We decided to have a closed-casket visitation. Then it wouldn't matter; no one would be the wiser, and everything could proceed on schedule. The director assured us we would have a private viewing for family members the morning after the funeral.

I wasn't sure how I really felt about seeing Donald's body. Part of me wanted confirmation, wanted to know beyond any doubt whether or not he was really gone, or whether some ghastly mistake had been made. Another part of me remembered all the loved ones I had seen in their caskets in the past, and I dreaded the thought of seeing my Donald lying there with no life left in him. I managed to find a stolen moment all to myself. I talked to Donald as if he was standing right next to me.

"I know you are happier now, Donald," I whispered, "but I miss you so much! I'm sorry I wasn't there with you. I'm sorry you were alone. I'm sorry for any of the times I was mean to you when we were kids. You are the best little brother in the entire world! Please, Donald, send me a sign that you're okay. I need one. Please send me a sign!"

At the visitation that evening, Richard and I were pleasantly surprised by the large number of people who attended. In his short life, Donald had touched many lives, and it was heartwarming to realize he had been important to many more people than just his family members. People who had known us since we were children came to pay their respects and honor my brother. Coworkers from both Colonial Williamsburg and Jamestown came. Childhood friends and old schoolmates came. Donald's publisher came. Even an old girlfriend came, and I never even knew she existed! The epiphany that my little brother had lived a fuller life than I even realized slowly sank in, and I was buoyed up by the knowledge of it.

The morning on the day of Donald's funeral dawned with a weak sun shining through a thin haze of wispy clouds intermitted with a pale blue sky. The forecast was calling for rain later on in the day. There was a crisp fall breeze, and I was glad for my sweater as we walked from our hotel building across the parking lot to the hotel's restaurant for breakfast. I felt drained and numb. I was just going through the motions. I didn't even acknowledge the taste of the food I ate.

When we had finished eating, George grabbed a *USA Today* from a newspaper vending machine, and we started walking back toward the hotel building. George grabbed my hand in his and asked me if I was okay. I nodded and rested my head against his shoulder as we walked. We approached the sidewalk running along next to the building, and then I had a sudden urge to look over at the tree-lined area on the opposite side of the parking lot. It was as though an invisible hand had tapped me on the shoulder. I gasped and stopped walking. My mouth dropped all the way open. "George," I said and grabbed his arm to stop him. "Look!" I pointed toward the tall pine trees. Sitting in the branches were several large black birds, perching in their familiar hunched-over position. Buzzards!

Dozens of them! "Look at that," George said softly as he watched them, almost mesmerized by them. "That's too weird to be a coincidence," he said. I smiled as I felt tears fill my eyes.

"No, that's no coincidence. It's Donald. He sent them. He sent me a sign just like I asked him to!"

Katie and Nicholas had noticed the birds and were talking in loud, excited voices. George and I ushered them into the hotel and up to the second floor to our room. Once inside, I rushed over to the large window and drew back the heavy drapes. The same tree-lined area was just outside our window, and we had a full, unobstructed view of the buzzards. There were many more now than when I had first spotted them. I counted fourteen perched in the trees and several more flying over, looking for a spot to land. "I have never seen so many vultures in one place at the same time in all my life!" George said, watching them. "Look, Mom! Here come some more!" Nicholas piped up.

I couldn't take my eyes off them. I felt tingly all over. I stared and stared out the window, a big smile across my face.

"This is so like Donald," I said. "He wanted to make sure I wouldn't miss this!" I could imagine him saying, *I'm not sending you one buzzard. You get a whole flock, just so there can be no mistake. I am okay! Don't worry about me!*

I grabbed my cell phone to call Richard. I had to tell him about this miraculous sign.

I watched the buzzards in the trees for a long time, over an hour. The final count was eighteen. They seemed contented to stay in the pine trees. They would stretch their wings and flap a bit and stare over toward us as we stared back. The only reason I stopped watching them was that we had to leave to go over to Richard's before the funeral. It was difficult for me to leave the window. Watching them was weirdly comforting. They weren't beautiful birds, but their meaning for me was significantly beautiful. I knew instinctively that when we returned to the hotel later, they would be gone. They had done their job, delivered their message, and would go back to doing what buzzards do naturally. Hanging out together in groups of eighteen was not natural for them.

By the time the funeral started at four o'clock, it had begun to rain. It felt like the whole world was crying for the loss of Donald. The skies were shades of dull gray, conjuring feelings of emptiness and hopelessness. Even the glow of candlelight in the church did nothing to warm my spirits. We had chosen a later hour for the service, hoping to allow working friends a greater opportunity to attend. The organ music was pleasant, *Sleepers, Wake* by J. S. Bach. I watched the raindrops run in rivulets down the glass panes of the tall windows. *Like a million tears*, I thought. I nervously fingered the paper I held with the words I had written about my brother. I was beginning to feel anxious about reading aloud. I remembered a time during my high school years when I had been asked by our minister to read a lesson aloud during a service. Reluctantly, I had agreed. I had been dreadfully nervous and had barely spoken loud enough for the congregation to hear my words. Now I *wanted* to speak, but like an old nemesis, my nerves were causing me trouble. Richard would speak first. For some reason, that made me feel more at ease.

When the time finally came, I listened to Richard and was awed by his remarks. His voice was strong and rich with raw emotion.

Watching him reminded me of Uncle Don when he preached. Richard had a similar spark. *That would please Momma*, I thought. Soon it was my turn. I fleetingly wondered if I could do Donald the same justice Richard had. I took deep breaths as I walked up to the podium. I took a moment to look out over the crowd. They were watching me. But it wasn't scary as it had been so many years before. The faces I saw were sympathetic and understanding. I smiled at them, and then I began.

I'd like to thank all of you for coming today. I wish it could be under happier circumstances. The last few days have been surreal— much like a bad dream as I try to wrap my mind around the fact that Donald is gone. In the midst of all the chaos of final preparations these last three days, I have had the strongest desire to see Donald suddenly burst through the door and yell, "Surprise!"

Many of us here today sat together in this church on a similar fall day twenty-two years ago. That was the day I began a mothering role of taking care of my two brothers. It is a job I have never felt burdened by and have taken on with the greatest joy. It was as natural as breathing.

That was also the day that Donald's search began. Those who know him well understand what I mean. Donald has been like a lost boy, looking for, and longing for, reasons why he was put on this earth. He wondered about and questioned what I have always known about him. He had a very important purpose on this earth. He was needed! Needed by our parents and needed by Richard and me much more than he probably ever realized. For so long, it has been the three of us against the world. Richard and I feel incomplete without him. He kept us down to earth, and we could always count on him. He lightened our load. He did that for others as well. Donald would have given you the shirt off his back if he thought it would have helped. He brightened a room with his smile, and he brought joy to all who knew him.

Our mother called him her "gentle giant." Our grandmother called him her "Don-boy."

Donald had a youthful spirit that enjoyed life, and his heart was as big as he was. He had strength of conviction and a strong sense of right from wrong. He was fiercely loyal to those he cared about. He had a great sense of humor and a quick wit. He was so, so brilliantly smart.

Though he had many struggles and disappointments in his life, he still accomplished a lot in his thirty-four years. He put himself through college and earned a degree in history. He fulfilled a lifelong dream by studying in London and touring all over England. Most impressive of all was that he researched, wrote, and had published a very detailed book about the weaponry of the period in history that fascinated him.

I don't have many regrets for what I did or didn't do for my brother. I have always been there for him when he needed me. I always told him I loved him more times than there are stars in the sky. And I always let him know how proud I am of him. My regrets are for him, and what he will never get to accomplish, and for how empty a piece of my heart will always be without him here. We will all miss his laughter and his big bear hugs.

But let us not dwell on the sadness of our loss. He would not want that. Today marks the end of Donald's search and a new beginning for his spirit. We must rejoice in the peace and happiness he has found at last.

I believe that in heaven there are a mother and a father walking hand in hand with a tall smiling son. It is a beautiful, sunny fall day, and a black-and-white border collie bounces along beside them as they walk down a path of falling golden leaves. They are laughing and talking together, full of joy in their reunion.

Donald will forever be young in our memories. He will always be our gentle giant with a hearty grin and a joke to tell. In the past days, I have been overwhelmed by the number of people who have shared their love of Donald with me. I never realized that so many people knew how special he truly was, but I am so very glad. We must keep him alive in our hearts and do as much as he did . . . LIVE WELL. LAUGH OFTEN. LOVE MUCH!

I won't say good-bye to you, Donald, because I know without a doubt that we will see each other again someday.

I did it. I said everything I had written, and I had done it well. George nodded his approval. I could see in his eyes that he was proud of me. I went back and sat next to him as the service continued.

After the final prayers were said, the six pallbearers went over to the casket. George was one of them. At the back of the church stood a single bagpiper wearing full Scottish dress uniform. He began playing "Amazing Grace" as the casket was carried out of the church. Family members followed behind. The steady rain and the mournful wail of the bagpipe tugged at my heart. But what got to me the most was the sight of my husband's face. Tears, not raindrops, streaked his cheeks as he held the casket. Then I noticed the faces of the others helping to carry the heavy casket over to the waiting hearse. They were visibly moved as well, perfect illustrations of grief and pain from the loss of a friend. It is a sight I will always remember.

The next morning dawned with sunshine again. The air smelled fresh and clean from the rain. We were packed and ready for our long drive back to Columbus. The only thing left to do was stop by the funeral home for the family viewing. George and Richard's wife, Susan, decided they didn't want to see the body. They both felt it would be too difficult for them. The children, we all agreed, were too young. Katie protested a bit. She wanted to see her Uncle Donald, and she reminded us that at twelve, she was not a baby any longer. I explained that it would be better if she remembered him as she knew him in life. "He won't look the same," I told her. "Trust me, I know." Katie frowned and scowled at me, but she didn't argue further. We left the children with Susan, and George drove Richard and me to the funeral home. We walked inside. It was eerily quiet. The garnet-colored carpet seemed to stretch for miles from the open foyer down a long hallway.

The director emerged suddenly from a door and welcomed us. He motioned to a door opposite the one he had come from and said for us to proceed on in when we were ready. George sat on a cushioned bench outside the door. "I'll wait for you here," he said. My heart seemed to be beating a path up from my chest into my throat. I didn't know exactly what to expect. The director opened the door to the room, and Richard and I walked inside. Then he closed the door behind us. The casket was situated on the far side of the room. Other than a wing chair and a floor lamp positioned near the door where we came in, the room had no other furniture. There was one window with gauzy curtains letting in filtered light. The casket sat opposite the window. Donald was not fully visible, lying in the casket, when we first entered the room. Richard approached first, and I followed. My eyes widened as Donald's body came into view. He was wearing the new charcoal gray suit Uncle Don had bought him, a white dress shirt, and a silk tie, with a little English crest pattern I recognized as one of his favorites. His face looked stiff, yet peaceful. His coloring was off, though. Gone was the healthy pink glow on the face speckled with freckles. He looked grayish; his freckles were pale. I was noticing the old scar on the right side of his mouth, an injury from long ago caused by our dog jumping up on him, when a piercing moan broke the heavy silence. It crescendoed into a piercing scream of pain and agony. Richard turned abruptly away from the casket and ran toward the wing chair at the other end of the room; crouched down, burying his head in its seat; and wept bitterly. I stood there, helpless, with my mouth agape, paralyzed by Richard's sudden reaction. How could I comfort him? I couldn't change any of this, no matter how badly I wanted to do so. I lifted my eyes toward the ceiling over the casket. "Donald," I whispered. "Help, me! Help me to help Richard. I don't know what to do!"

I turned toward the chair and went over to Richard. "It's okay, Rich," I said soothingly. "You don't have to stay in here if you don't want to." To my relief, he stood up. "I'm sorry," he whispered hoarsely, gathering himself. "This is just harder than I ever imagined. Seeing him makes it so final." I nodded my head in agreement. We walked back over to the casket a second time, arm in arm. Richard patted Donald's shoulder, and I watched him with envy. I wanted to touch Donald too. But that old fear was taunting me at the back of my mind. I had never touched Momma or Daddy in their caskets. I was determined not to let fear get the better of me this time. I reached out my hand. I couldn't bring myself to touch any exposed skin. I rested my hand on his arm. It felt hard like cement under the wool of his suit, not soft and fleshy. I felt shocked at this revelation. It was just a further confirmation that Donald was truly gone. I did not pull my hand away immediately. I lingered for a moment, patting my brother and whispering, "I love you, Donny boy. I'll love you forever."

EPILOGUE

We often hear that time heals all wounds. From my experiences, this is not exactly true. I have found that there are times when the wounds from loss are distant, quiet, and easily pushed aside. But it doesn't take much, and in an instant, they can renew strength like a hurricane churning in warm waters. Often it happens when you least expect it. The old pain can be exposed again and can tear at your heart as though the loss just happened. Holidays are never quite the same. Important milestone events barely make the hallmark moments you always dreamed about. My parents missed it all: graduations, weddings, work promotions, births, christenings, and worst of all, knowing their grandchildren. I don't believe you can *ever* heal from the loss of a loved one. There is always a longing and an ache whether you choose to acknowledge it or not. I *do* think you can learn to pick up the pieces of your life and move on. You will never forget those you have lost, but you can move forward. It is a choice you make. You decide how to handle what life throws at you. Many times over the years, people have remarked upon hearing my story, "How did you ever get through that?" How, indeed?

It is a tricky thing to keep the memory of a loved one alive without allowing yourself to become stuck in the past. I prefer to celebrate their lives and not dwell on their deaths. Family pictures are important, as well as family traditions and sharing stories of past days. When Richard and I get our families together, our children love to hear stories of funny things we did as kids. Richard has a special talent for reenacting a selection of hilarious tales from our childhood.

It reminds me of times when I was little and listened to Uncle Don or Uncle B., telling stories about Momma. Life comes full circle. Time may not heal all wounds, but it has a way of softening the rough edges, like running water smoothing sharp rocks into pebbles

I have always felt that I have a special purpose in this world. I always want to do more, to help more, to see more, and to make things better. I know that life can dole out some pretty tough cards, but I also know that you can get through it and not fall apart. You just pick up, and you keep going. The answers to this survival technique are so simple and so basic. Love and faith. The love my parents had for each other blanketed us, their children, like a sheltering umbrella. Momma and Daddy gave us unconditional love. They loved us no matter what we did or said, whether we were good or bad or in between. My mother always told me, "You can do anything, Elizabeth, if you just put your mind to it." When you are loved and supported like that, it sustains you. It makes you feel strong enough to make it through anything. It gives you the faith to know you *can* make it through anything. When I was a little girl, I always liked the story of Noah's Ark. I especially liked the part where Noah saw the dove carrying the olive branch in its mouth and the beautiful rainbow arching across the sky. The olive branch was a sign of hope and of love. Noah knew that God still loved him and every creature left on earth. I believe love can do that for *anyone*. During her illness, my mother's love was like an olive branch to her family, telling us that we could go on after she died because her love for us would *never* die. This book is full of the miracles of love. Miracles don't have to occur with fireworks and grand applause. They happen every day in the quiet strength of a loved one who lives one more day despite a doctor's bleak diagnosis, in the sudden appearance of a butterfly, or a feather, or a coin that shows up in an unexpected place. You have to keep your eyes open. You have to keep your mind open as well. I never would have imagined that one day I would revel in the sight of a vulture soaring high in the sky, and find great beauty and majesty in its expansive wing spread silhouetted against the blue sky!

I know that people endure sad losses like mine every day. September 11 and the Iraq War have created many children who suffer from the loss of one or both parents. Families have been torn apart; siblings are lost and sons and daughters too. I know how much that can hurt, and I want more than anything to be able to bring hope and healing to others by sharing my story. I have seen proof that love lives on and never dies. I know in my heart that death is not the end of us, but a beginning of a new life in another realm. They will send you signs that they still exist if you are willing to look for them. And though you may hurt from the loss of a loved one, celebrate the life and love that you shared with them and find the determination to go on. You must surround yourself with *love*. Let it be your olive branch.

Printed in the United States
221615BV00001B/72/P